D1243332

Economic Relations in the Asian-Pacific Region

Brookings Dialogues on Public Policy

The presentations and discussions at Brookings conferences and seminars often deserve wide circulation as contributions to public understanding of issues of national importance. The Brookings Dialogues on Public Policy series is intended to make such statements and commentary available to a broad and general audience, usually in summary form. The series supplements the Institution's research publications by reflecting the contrasting, often lively, and sometimes conflicting views of elected and appointed government officials, other leaders in public and private life, and scholars. In keeping with their origin and purpose, the Dialogues are not subjected to the formal review procedures established for the Institution's research publications. Brookings publishes them in the belief that they are worthy of public consideration but does not assume responsibility for their accuracy or objectivity. And, as in all Brookings publications, the judgments, conclusions, and recommendations presented in the Dialogues should not be ascribed to the trustees, officers, or other staff members of the Brookings Institution.

Economic Relations in the Asian-Pacific Region

EDITED BY

Bruce Dickson & Harry Harding

report of a conference cosponsored by the Chinese Academy of Social Sciences and the Brookings Institution, June 1985

THE BROOKINGS INSTITUTION
Washington, D.C.

Copyright © 1987 by
THE BROOKINGS INSTITUTION
1775 Massachusetts Avenue, N.W.
Washington, D.C. 20036

Library of Congress Catalog Card Number 86-72739
ISBN 0-8157-1841-1

9 8 7 6 5 4 3 2 1

DISCARDED
WIDENER UNIVERSITY

WIDENER UNIVERSITY
WOLFGRAM
LIBRARY
CHESTER, PA.

About Brookings

Board of Trustees
Louis W. Cabot
Chairman
Ralph S. Saul
Vice Chairman;
Chairman, Executive Committee
Chairman, Development Committee
Samuel H. Armacost
J. David Barnes
Rex J. Bates
Frank T. Cary
A. W. Clausen
William T. Coleman, Jr.
Lloyd N. Cutler
Thomas R. Donahue
Charles W. Duncan, Jr.
Walter Y. Elisha
Robert F. Erburu
Roberto C. Goizueta
Robert D. Haas
Philip M. Hawley
Amory Houghton, Jr.
Roy M. Huffington
B. R. Inman
Vernon E. Jordan, Jr.
James A. Joseph
James T. Lynn
Donald F. McHenry
Bruce K. MacLaury
Mary Patterson McPherson
Donald S. Perkins
J. Woodward Redmond
James D. Robinson III
Robert V. Roosa
Henry B. Schacht
Howard R. Swearer
Morris Tanenbaum
James D. Wolfensohn
Ezra K. Zilkha
Charles J. Zwick
Honorary Trustees
Vincent M. Barnett, Jr.
Barton M. Biggs
Eugene B. Black
Robert D. Calkins
Edward W. Carter
Bruce B. Dayton
Douglas Dillon
Huntington Harris
Andrew Heiskell
Roger W. Heyns
John E. Lockwood
William McC. Martin, Jr.
Robert S. McNamara
Arjay Miller
Charles W. Robinson
H. Chapman Rose
Gerard C. Smith
Robert Brookings Smith
Sydney Stein, Jr.
Phyllis A. Wallace

THE BROOKINGS INSTITUTION is a private nonprofit organization devoted to research, education, and publication in economics, government, foreign policy, and the social sciences generally. Its principal purpose is to bring knowledge to bear on the current and emerging public policy problems facing the American people. In its research, Brookings functions as an independent analyst and critic, committed to publishing its findings for the information of the public. In its conferences and other activities, it serves as a bridge between scholarship and public policy, bringing new knowledge to the attention of decisionmakers and affording scholars a better insight into policy issues. Its activities are carried out through three research programs (Economic Studies, Governmental Studies, Foreign Policy Studies), a Center for Public Policy Education, a Publications Program, and a Social Science Computation Center.

The Institution was incorporated in 1927 to merge the Institute for Government Research, founded in 1916 as the first private organization devoted to public policy issues at the national level; the Institute of Economics, established in 1922 to study economic problems; and the Robert Brookings Graduate School of Economics and Government, organized in 1924 as a pioneering experiment in training for public service. The consolidated institution was named in honor of Robert Somers Brookings (1850–1932), a St. Louis businessman whose leadership shaped the earlier organizations.

Brookings is financed largely by endowment and by the support of philanthropic foundations, corporations, and private individuals. Its funds are devoted to carrying out its own research and educational activities. It also undertakes some unclassified government contract studies, reserving the right to publish its findings.

A Board of Trustees is responsible for general supervision of the Institution, approval of fields of investigation, and safeguarding the independence of the Institution's work. The President is the chief administrative officer, responsible for formulating and coordinating policies, recommending projects, approving publications, and selecting the staff.

Editors' Preface

IN EARLY June 1985, the Brookings Institution and the Chinese Academy of Social Sciences cosponsored a conference entitled "Economic Relations in the Asian-Pacific Region: Trends and Prospects." This was the third in an ongoing series of joint conferences organized by the two institutions. The first, held in Williamsburg, Virginia, in 1981, considered political and security matters in Asia. The second, which took place in Peking, in 1982, examined global economic problems.

The most recent conference, convened at the Wye Plantation in eastern Maryland, considered the economic policies and prospects of key countries and territories in the Asian-Pacific region and the impact of those internal developments on important economic relationships in the region. In a sense, the Wye conference served to integrate the topics of the first two meetings—Asia and economics—into a single agenda.

The Wye conference brought together twelve scholars from the United States and nine scholars from the People's Republic of China who shared an interest in trade patterns and economic trends in the Pacific Basin. A list of the participants and of the papers presented at the conference appears at the end of this volume. Four sessions of the conference focused on the economic policies of the primary Pacific economic actors: the United States, China, Japan, and the newly industrialized countries of East and Southeast Asia. Two of the most important types of commodities involved in Asian-Pacific trade were also considered: labor-intensive manufactures and advanced technology. At a final, less structured session, participants discussed the implications of the conference findings for Sino-American economic relations and for economic cooperation in the Asian-Pacific region.

Like its predecessors, the Wye conference was a valuable and effective way of introducing Chinese scholars to the methodologies and conclusions of American social science, building contacts between American scholars and their counterparts in China, and, above all, exchanging opinions and perspectives on policy-related

vii

issues of vital interest to both countries. The relaxed setting of the Wye Plantation facilitated a candid and lively discussion. Indeed, the disagreements voiced within each delegation were almost as stark as the differences between the Chinese scholars and their American colleagues.

The discussions at Wye were so fruitful that we at Brookings feel it appropriate to share the results with a wider audience. It is our hope that the views expressed in this book will not only capture the views of a specific moment, but will also reflect the more enduring economic developments in China and the rest of the Asian-Pacific region, indicate some important trends in recent Chinese scholarship, and symbolize the expanding academic dialogue between China and the United States.

This book weaves together excerpts from the formal papers presented at the conference with paraphrases of the comments made during the subsequent discussions. Excerpts from the papers are identified by the name of the author. Because the conference was off the record, however, the paraphrases of the oral remarks show only the nationality of the speaker. We are solely responsible for selecting the excerpts and for the paraphrasing of the comments made at the conference.

The result is a revealing international dialogue, organized around the central themes that dominated the discussions. First, we consider the prospects for the export-oriented economies of East Asia, the impact of Japanese and American economic policies on regional growth, and the threat of protectionism to regional trade. Second, we offer a detailed review of China's dramatic economic reform program and its "open economy" policy and assess the likely impact of these developments on neighboring countries, particularly Japan. We conclude with a brief discussion of the prospects for cooperation and dialogue in the Asian-Pacific region and for Sino-American relations.

The Brookings Institution is grateful to the Ford Foundation, the Rockefeller Brothers Fund, and the Committee on International Relations Studies with the People's Republic of China for financial support of the conference. A post-conference tour for the Chinese delegation, conducted by the National Committee on U.S.-China Relations, was sponsored by the U.S. Information Agency. Julia Sternberg and Susan Nichols provided organizational and secretarial assistance. Theresa Walker edited the manuscript.

December 1986   Bruce Dickson
Washington, D.C.   Harry Harding

Contents

Regional Economic Trends   **1**

  Prospects for the Developing Economies of East Asia   1
  Impact of the Japanese and American Economies   11
  North-South Relations and Protectionism   27

China's Reforms and the Future   **39**

  The Domestic Reforms   39
  The "Open Economy" Policy   54
  Implications for the Region   73

**Implications for Relations between the United States
and China**   **81**

  The Expansion of Trade   81
  Political Dimensions   86

Conference Participants   **90**

Regional Economic Trends

IN AN analysis of the general pattern of economic relations in the Asian-Pacific region, many members of the Chinese delegation strongly criticized what they perceived as growing protectionist sentiment in the United States. They urged the United States to keep its markets open to absorb the exports that China hopes will finance the purchase of advanced foreign technology. Many American participants, however, felt that their Chinese colleagues applied a double standard to the issue of protectionism, in that they criticized the United States and other developed countries for restricting imports, while defending the right of China and other developing countries to do the same. The opinion of most of the American scholars was that the North-South dialogue must produce reciprocal trade concessions, whereby both developed and developing countries agree to open their markets to goods and services from abroad. The Chinese participants did not accept this viewpoint but argued that the protection of infant industries in developing countries differed in purpose and outcome from the protection of older, inefficient industries in more advanced nations.

Prospects for the Developing Economies of East Asia

Excerpt from the paper by Lawrence B. Krause

THE DEVELOPING countries of the Asian-Pacific region began to significantly outperform other less developed countries (LDCs) during the difficult economic period after 1973. In these years a series of economic disturbances, including a sharp jump in oil prices in 1973–74, a normal cyclical recovery, a second rise in oil prices, a sharp increase in interest rates, a prolonged and deep worldwide recession, a debt crisis for LDCs, and now an atypical recovery affected all countries. The impact of these forces upon different countries depended in part on their productive structures and in part on their policy responses to the disturbances. The experience of this region seems to suggest that the countries of East and Southeast Asia are more adaptable than countries else-

1

where. This particular "comparative advantage" is most valuable during periods of severe economic disturbance.

For one thing, the good economic performance of Japan, especially in earlier years, has had beneficial spillover effects on its neighbors in the Pacific Basin. For example, Japan bought raw materials, transferred technology, and provided some capital and tourists, which in turn enhanced growth prospects for other countries.

However, these spillover effects could not have occurred if the other countries in the region had not been open to foreign influences. Compared with developing countries in other parts of the world, the LDCs in East and Southeast Asia have introduced more outward-oriented policies. Thus it is not by accident that these countries have maintained rapid growth of exports and have a high ratio of trade to gross national product (GNP). Singapore and Hong Kong are at the extreme of conducting completely free trade practices. A policy of liberalizing imports as one ingredient of an export-led growth strategy has been followed since the early 1960s in Taiwan and the mid-1960s in South Korea. The countries of the Association of Southeast Asian Nations (ASEAN) that export natural resources do maintain some protection for manufactures, which ranges from moderate in Malaysia to fairly restrictive in Indonesia. However, the protection is comparatively less strong than in LDCs elsewhere with similar economic structures and stages of development. None of the countries of ASEAN envisions its development in a context of self-sufficiency. Instead these countries maintain an outward orientation.

The better economic performance of these East Asian countries is also enhanced by their pattern of trade concentration in the Pacific Basin. Two distinct patterns emerge. The newly industrialized countries (NICs) specialize in manufactured goods and sell from 50 percent to 70 percent of their exports within the Pacific Basin. The United States is by far their largest market. The other LDCs export primarily natural resources and sell from 50 percent to 80 percent of their exports within the Pacific Basin. For them, Japan is the largest market. Thus, regardless of specialization, the Pacific Basin provides a major market for these countries. The rapidly growing intra-LDC trade in the region, possibly enhanced by ASEAN, also forms part of the picture.

While not directly related to international trade, several other factors can help to explain the region's relative economic success. One consideration relates to economic ideology. All of the governments and their societies have been prepared to take a market-oriented approach to their economic development consistent with classical economic principles. Their labor markets reflect this approach. Artificial devices to push up money wages have generally been avoided, and wages have risen only in response to real labor scarcities. In addition, while permitting foreign economic influences to enter their countries, the host countries still maintain control. Classical economic principles also played a part in keeping these countries from becoming excessively indebted to foreign banks, a problem that has bedeviled other LDCs.

These countries have also adopted governmental policies that emphasize the promotion of economic growth and either ignore or pay less attention to distribution issues. They have concentrated on ways to facilitate industrial catch-up. In some countries, such as Singapore and South Korea, this emphasis has led to an active, almost intrusive, role for the government. In Hong Kong, by contrast, the government achieved the same objective by leaving private enterprises alone to manage by their own devices. Promoting growth often meant accepting market signals, such as maintaining a realistic exchange rate. Moreover, as one country first stated growth as a government objective and then achieved it, other neighboring countries followed suit.

Furthermore, it appears that private entrepreneurs were available in these societies to seize opportunities. Some observers have noted the great importance of overseas Chinese as entrepreneurs throughout the region. Only South Korea is an exception, but it too has strong Chinese cultural roots. Although it is not clear whether entrepreneurial instincts or a system of family ties is most significant in raising capital for new ventures, it is apparent that an important cultural pattern is clearly at work.

Finally, the political systems of these countries have been marked by general stability. When this stability has been shattered, such as in South Korea in 1980 or in the Philippines recently, the economy has suffered. Political stability promotes economic advance by reducing uncertainty and by encouraging saving and forward planning. However, the stability can be sustained only when a society builds a consensus on goals and priorities, which is accomplished through various institutional devices in each country.

The entire region is aware of the importance of international trade to continued prosperity and is greatly concerned by the specter of protectionism. Protectionism has been rising and if this trend is continued for much longer, it could undermine economic prosperity. The best way to prevent protectionism is actively to promote a more liberal and open trade system. Thus the countries in the region support a new round of the General Agreement on Tariffs and Trade (GATT) negotiations and view GATT as the best hope for achieving more open markets and simultaneously guarding against renewed protectionist threats.

Excerpt from the paper by Gu Yuanyang

DURING THE past forty years, significant economic development has occurred in East and Southeast Asia. Even when the West was experiencing stagflation and serious economic crisis, many countries and areas in the region were able to maintain a certain momentum in their economic development.

The direct manifestation of the sustained economic growth in East and Southeast Asia is the steady increase of per capita GNP. In 1984, the per capita GNP of Brunei exceeded $12,000 (U.S.), and it was $6,500 for Singapore, $5,000 for Hong Kong, $3,000 for Taiwan, nearly $2,000 for South Korea, $1,857 for Malaysia, $805 for Thailand, $720 for the Philippines, and $580 for Indonesia.[1]

To be sure, the polarization of wealth among the people and the enlarged income differentials between town and country have become a common social problem in East and Southeast Asia. Despite this problem, the development and prosperity of these regions have attracted the attention of people in many countries and have tempted them to find the reasons behind them. In my view, many factors are responsible for the sustained medium-to-high economic growth rate of East and Southeast Asia, but the main reason lies in the strategies and policies they have formulated and implemented in the course of their economic development. The emerging NICs and regions in Asia lack natural resources and have small markets. But, drawing on the experience of the Western countries after World War II, they have stressed investment in human resources and gradually attained superiority in this aspect. Combining this superiority with Western capital and technology, they have developed export-oriented processing industries with imported materials, turned out semifinished products, and assembled spare parts, generally by imitating and creating quality products. Thus these countries and areas, though latecomers, have surpassed the old-timers in the international market.

Despite past achievements, the engine of economic development in East and Southeast Asia—that is, the strategy in which trade plays a leading role in promoting economic development—is faced

1. *Asian Wall Street Journal,* October 22, 1984.

with many troubles. First of all, in the days to come, the rate of increase of world trade will not surpass that of the 1960s or 1970s. Second, because the Western countries have adopted a policy by which they want to ensure economic recovery on the one hand and keep the inflation rate low on the other, there will be a lower rate of economic growth in the future. Third, against a background of big deficits and high rates of unemployment, Western countries, the United States in particular, will place even harsher restrictions on imports from developing countries. Finally, the economic recovery of Western countries has not helped the prices of primary products to pick up. Instead, it has resulted in "nonsynchronistic" growth of the economy and prices. Low-speed economic growth and the new technological revolution will make it difficult for prices of commodities to rise significantly. East and Southeast Asia can neither control nor influence these and other external forces that limit economic growth. Their outward-oriented economic policies and strategies for economic development have resulted in a "pan bottom" economy, which is quick to heat up and quick to cool down. When there is an economic boom and brisk demand in the West, then East Asia will enjoy increased exports, leading to economic growth. But when their exports dwindle, the East Asian countries and regions will encounter a recession throughout their economy.

The rate of economic development in East and Southeast Asia from the late 1980s until the end of this century will depend on whether or not the economic policies practiced now will continue to be effective, and on whether their structural readjustments will be successful in resolving the various internal and external contradictions, economic or noneconomic in nature, that these countries encounter. At present, the newly industrialized countries and areas in Asia are faced with several threats. First, the competitiveness of labor-intensive products manufactured in the region has been gradually reduced in the world market as a result of increases in the wages of workers and in the costs of production. These goods may be displaced by products from other developing countries. Second, by combining their electronic technology with engineering technology the developed countries have turned from mechanization to automation, rejuvenating some traditional industries and increasing the threat to Asian labor-intensive exports. Furthermore, the Western developed countries are imposing more and more restrictions on the labor-intensive products exported by East and Southeast Asian countries and areas. Faced with these pressures, the newly industrialized countries and areas in Asia began their "second industrial revolution" or "industrial updating" in the mid-1970s, with the aim of switching from labor-intensive industries to technology- and knowledge-intensive industries and from a strategy of "building up the country by means of export trade" to a strategy of "building up the country by means of high technology." To this end, they have taken a greater interest in importing advanced equipment and technology, carrying out research, increasing investments in new industries, setting up scientific-industrial centers, and developing highly technology-intensive and low energy-intensive industries that turn out products with high added value and with very little pollution.

The economic recession in the Western countries and the falling off of prices of raw materials have adversely affected the ASEAN countries because they are increasingly dependent on the Western developed countries. In reforming their economic policies and readjusting their industrial structure, they have to rely mainly on foreign capital, equipment, and technology to establish and develop their own industrial system based on domestic products. But, by rejuvenating some traditional industries and developing new industries, they hope to remedy gradually their lopsided economic structure.

If East and Southeast Asia carry out this reform and readjustment smoothly, the adverse effects imposed on them by the world economy will be reduced. They will be in a better position to seek a new opportunity of survival through scientific and technological advances and development in the face of ever fiercer competition in the world. They have already made some progress in the reform and readjustment of their economies. If this trend continues, then by the end of this century the average economic growth rate in East and Southeast Asia could reach 4 percent to 5 percent or even 5 percent to 6 percent. Though that cannot match the figure in the 1960s or 1970s, East and Southeast Asia will then become the new center of production and trade in the world.

However, the readjustment and change of industrial structure and trade patterns in Asia is no easy job. The creation of new industries and the updating of other ones will still have to rely largely on equipment and technology imported from the United States, Japan, and other developed countries, as well as on access to their markets. If the developed countries fear the enhanced competitiveness of the developing Asian-Pacific countries, they may take no interest or even actively stand in the way of the economic reform and readjustment of the less-advanced parts of the region. If that happens, it will be difficult for these countries and areas to realize their ambitious objectives of development. The prospects for future economic growth in East and Southeast Asia, a bright spot in the gloomy picture of the world economy, will surely dim. Clearly, the North-South question is of vital importance for East and Southeast Asia. In predicting the prospects for economic development in these regions, it is necessary to study the present state and the future possible development of North-South relations in Asia.

Excerpt from the paper by Wang Zengzhuang

How is it that the Asian-Pacific region has developed so fast? Its success is often attributed to rich human and natural resources, but these factors are peripheral to sustained development rather than the key to high economic growth. In fact, countries and areas poor in natural resources took the lead in attaining such expansion. Evidently, one of the most important contributing factors is the importation and application of advanced technology. By absorbing foreign capital and technology, the developing Asian-Pacific countries and areas have acquired much-wanted production techniques and managerial skills at a relatively low cost, whereas they themselves have the necessary capabilities for absorbing and applying such techniques and skills, thus attaining quick economic growth. Such is the path Japan has taken, and the developing Asian-Pacific countries and areas are still in this process.

The export-oriented development strategy based on importing foreign capital and technologies and expanding foreign trade has also brought many problems to the economies of the developing Asian-Pacific countries and regions. For instance, quite a few countries and areas lean so heavily upon foreign trade, with their external economic relations centering so much around the United States and Japan, that their economies are susceptible to many destabilizing factors, such as the adverse impact of the economic crises in the capitalist world and the control and maneuvering by American and Japanese multinational corporations. Problems of this kind deserve close attention, though they have not yet seriously affected economic development. Given their proper solution, the economies of these countries will continue to develop at a fairly fast rate.

The new technological revolution centering on microelectronics, which is emerging on a global scale, is providing new opportunities for the economic development of the Asian-Pacific region. The United States and Japan will maintain their lead in new scientific discoveries and breakthroughs. But the close economic ties between the developing Asian-Pacific countries and areas on the one hand, and the United States and Japan on the other, make it quite feasible for new technologies to be transferred from the latter to the former. As a result, the developing Asian-Pacific countries and areas are likely to be among the greatest beneficiaries of this new technological revolution. They have a considerable industrial base, abundant intellectual resources, and the capacity to absorb new technology and train the necessary specialized personnel.

However, the new technological revolution will cause certain problems in the economies of developing Asian-Pacific countries and areas. First, the new technological revolution will bring forth numerous new industries and new products and thus change the patterns of the international market so that the demands of developed countries for traditional labor-intensive products that are low in manufacturing technique will decrease gradually to the point of market saturation. Second, owing to the application of new technologies, such as microelectronics and robots, certain traditional industries that have been phased out in the developed countries will begin to come back and cause these countries to adopt protectionist measures against competition of similar products from developing countries and areas. Third, as labor-intensive industries use not only a great deal of labor but also much energy and raw materials, the fairly rapid increase in labor costs in these countries and areas and the greatly inflated prices of petroleum and other imported raw materials will raise the overall costs of their products, making them less and less competitive.

Confronted with these problems, the developing Asian-Pacific countries and areas, especially Singapore, South Korea, Taiwan province, and Hong Kong, began in the late 1970s or early 1980s to take countermeasures aimed at restructuring their industries toward greater sophistication and diversification, with the development of electronics as their core. Viewed from a historical perspective, it is only a matter of time until the new technological revolution and the trends of industrial restructuring in Singapore, South Korea, Taiwan province, and Hong Kong engulf the other ASEAN countries.

Comments

AMERICAN PARTICIPANT. If the international environment worsens, should the East Asian countries change their policies of outward-oriented growth? I feel that even in a hostile environment, an outward orientation is more beneficial than an inward-looking one.

AMERICAN PARTICIPANT. Emphasizing only internal factors and the international trading system as a whole ignores regional considerations. Countries in the region are engaged in a process of defining their comparative advantage relative to one another to maintain a viable strategy for exports. What are the prospects for their doing so? What impact will China have on regional trading patterns?

Excerpt from the paper by Wang Dingyong

THE IMPORT-EXPORT trade among developing countries has an important place in the trade relations of the Asian-Pacific region. In particular, the development of trade relations between China and other developing countries and areas will have a profound impact on the trade structure in this region. It is true that, owing to the rising wage levels in the newly industrialized areas, their export of labor-intensive products faces competition of the same products from the ASEAN countries and China. However, the crux of the matter is not competition, but markets. If markets develop and expand, competition will help improve the quality of products and raise technical levels. The trade protectionism of the advanced countries constitutes the biggest obstacle to the export of labor-intensive products of the developing countries and regions.

Excerpt from the paper by Charles S. Pearson

THE COUNTRIES of the Asian-Pacific region exhibit a dynamic process of changing comparative advantage. The essential feature, apart from rapid overall growth of manufactured exports, appears to be the changing structure of manufactured exports. A useful analogy may be that countries are at different rungs and moving up a product sophistication ladder, with labor-intensive, capital-intensive, and technology-intensive products at the lower, middle, and upper rungs, respectively. Alternatively, one can view export products as moving down a country ladder, as, for example, the shift of labor-intensive products away from Japan in the 1950s and early 1960s, first toward the Asian NICs and more recently and speculatively toward the ASEAN countries.

One way to test the ladder analogy is to measure changes in countries' shares of world trade by commodity. This approach, however, may be misleading if one country's total exports grow more rapidly than another's. Measuring the share of a commodity in a single country's export of manufactures is an alternative. These shares can then be recast as a similarity index and used to compare countries at the same time and their levels of development over time. The calculation of export similarity indexes reveals that the ASEAN countries emphasize resource-intensive exports, while the NICs depend on labor-intensive manufactures. Taiwan and South Korea still rely on traditional exports (for example, clothes and toys) even though they have gained a foothold in more advanced products. The index is also useful for ranking countries by the sophistication of their export structure: the United States and Japan at the top, then the Asian NICs, and ASEAN (with Singapore as a maverick) at the bottom. China falls between the NICs and ASEAN. Japan is catching up with the United States, and Taiwan and South Korea are tracking Japan's earlier pattern but have so far been unable to catch up with a moving target. The NICs are moving up the ladder but not as fast as originally thought because they are lingering in traditional industries. China's development will encounter pressure from below by countries with similar exports and from above by developed countries that protect their markets. The entry of China into the international economy will encourage the NICs to vacate the lower rungs on the ladder of product sophistication.

It appears that the Asian NICs have moved up the product ladder slowly, maintaining a position on the "traditional products" rung, while also securing a position in nontraditional manufactures at higher rungs. One explanation for this slow movement may be that countries have become adept at upgrading to higher value-added products within the same product category, thereby increasing the skill and capital intensity of what appear to be traditional manufactures.

Comments

CHINESE PARTICIPANT. There is currently a sorting out of comparative advantage in the Asian-Pacific region. I agree with Pearson's theory of ladders, but there is no absolute correlation between a country's place on the ladder and the products it exports. Auto production is an example. The United States and Japan are different from Southeast Asia because the United States and Japan use their own technology to manufacture cars, while the Southeast Asian countries import their technology. Similarly, the heading "labor intensive" now includes electronic and consumer goods, not just textiles and clothes. The same product can be manufactured by different technologies in different countries.

CHINESE PARTICIPANT. Economic development cannot be explained by the ladder model because development is often unbalanced. If the trade of the developing countries follows Pearson's ladder there should be little competition with the developed countries, but in fact there is a lot of competition between Asian and American products. As the United States produces more technology-intensive goods, it should import greater amounts of labor-intensive goods, but the United States is placing more restrictions in this area. This is the problem with the model in theory and practice. Furthermore, in the future some countries may not follow the ladder model but may skip a few rungs and develop faster, and some countries may even drop from the top rung to a lower rung. Therefore, the law of development is imbalance, not the ladder model.

CHINESE PARTICIPANT. Is it possible for a country on the third rung (where ASEAN is said to be) to move directly to the second rung (where the newly industrialized countries and areas now stand), or even to the first rung? I believe it is possible, depending on the policies adopted. I think it is possible for some of the ASEAN countries, such as Indonesia and Malaysia, to move ahead of the newly industrialized countries and areas in the next few years. If their domestic policies conform with the international environment, it is possible to quicken the pace of development. Malaysia's rate of growth is higher than that of Hong Kong, Taiwan, and South Korea, and Indonesia is about the same. The ladder theory is interesting, but many countries may skip a rung.

AMERICAN PARTICIPANT. A country cannot skip a rung, and it is a mistake for them to try. However, it is possible to move up the ladder faster and even to pass another country. Rapid training of the labor force is required for the movement to the next rung. Korea tried to get prematurely into heavy and petrochemical industries in the 1970s and now exports a lot of those kinds of goods, but Korean companies still make most of their money through textiles and shoes because they have not gained the necessary production and marketing techniques to move up to the next rung.

Impact of the Japanese and American Economies

Excerpt from the paper by He Fang

SINCE THE BEGINNING of the 1980s, there have been two noteworthy changes in Japan, which has long become a so-called great economic power. One is the internationalization of the Japanese yen. This may facilitate Japan's financing activities, enliven its economy, and increase its competitiveness. On the other hand, this may also cause a free inflow and outflow of floating capital, which may weaken the government's power to control foreign exchange and the capital market. The other development is the sharp increase in Japan's trade surplus and export of capital. This, of course, may further enhance Japan's position in the world economy. However, the huge export surplus inevitably increases trade friction with other countries, and the substantial outflow of funds may harm domestic investment and economic growth. This may make Japan follow the same road that the United States took after World War II. In fact, Japan is now replacing the United States as the biggest creditor nation and capital exporting nation in the world.

Japan has paid constant attention to reestablishing or expanding sources of raw material and export markets in such areas as Southeast Asia, South Korea, China's Taiwan province, and Hong Kong. By the middle of the 1960s, Japan was able to break into these countries and regions economically through "war indemnities" and trade expansion. Later, the rapid growth of the Japanese economy made it more necessary to develop foreign economic relations. And these countries and regions were also in urgent need of expanding export and importing foreign capital to develop their own economy. That is why at the beginning of the 1980s Japan's volume of import and export trade with these countries and regions caught up with and surpassed that of the United States. Its direct investment also jumped to the first place. Such economic relations not only provided conditions for the growth of the Japanese economy, but also promoted economic development in these countries and regions.

Such relations were not all plain sailing, however. For example, the ASEAN nations were constantly complaining that Japan was too stingy in its transfer of technology, that its export policy was too "aggressive," that its imports were subject to rigid restrictions, and that its trade concessions were mainly granted to developed nations. The basic reason for this situation is that in the past, Japan only kept its eyes on acquiring resources, markets, and places for investment, without any regard for the needs of less-developed countries. What is more, Japanese aggression in the 1930s and 1940s still remained fresh in people's memory. Therefore, a general anti-Japan movement broke out in Asia at the end of the 1970s. At the beginning of the 1980s, Japan speeded up its work to win over these countries and tried to be as flexible as it possibly could. Its economic relations with the developing nations of the Asian-Pacific region may continue to develop, but contradictions will be hard to avoid.

Excerpt from the paper by Edward Lincoln

BESIDES HAVING played a positive role in Asia as a trader, Japan has also been a net investor: 27 percent of its direct foreign investment has been in Asia. The amount of its technology transfer has grown, and 40 percent of this amount has been to countries in the region. Japan has been a major foreign aid donor, with 70 percent of its bilateral aid in the 1980s being spent in the region. Its primary problem is that its macroeconomic policies have created a large current account surplus, and Japan is now stuck with the image of a reluctant importer.

It is true that, in the early postwar period, the Japanese government erected very high trade barriers, including both strict quotas and high tariffs. But beginning in the early 1960s, a process of dismantling these barriers began that is still continuing. Consequently, barriers to imports in Japan on average are relatively low. Some markets are quite open to imports while others remain rather heavily protected.

The economic developments of the past decade have placed two conflicting sets of pressures on Japan's trade policy. First, the emergence of surplus savings within the domestic economy and the rise of current account surpluses to accommodate the flow of those savings overseas have led to increased pressure from abroad to reduce import barriers. The overall current account surpluses have meant large bilateral merchandise trade surpluses with a number of key trading partners, especially the United States. Foreigners have repeatedly used the size of the trade imbalance as a reason why Japan should make concessions on import barriers. The argument can be put in one of two ways: either Japan is accused of having a surplus because of the restrictions on imports, or Japan is told that nations with large trade surpluses should be the leaders of the liberal trade regime. The first argument is clearly incorrect; Japan's surpluses are not caused by import barriers but rather by macroeconomic adjustments. However, the second argument is a legitimate one; Japan's image abroad is damaged by the impression it gives of being reluctant to reduce import barriers.

Given its international image as a recalcitrant member of the trading community, the policy problem facing the Japanese government is serious. Japan, like many countries, is rather inward looking and does not willingly sacrifice the particular interests of domestic producers to the abstract goal of a liberal international trade regime. However, the anger and frustration that this resistance has produced abroad has become serious enough to jeopardize the framework of the overall trading system. The Japanese response to date has been to recognize when foreign frustration is serious enough to result in retaliation against Japanese exports, and then Japan makes concessions. But this mode of behavior has done nothing to improve the international perception of Japan as a reluctant importer. Each round of this pattern worsens Japan's image in the United States, bringing closer the possibility of harsh retaliation. By the spring of 1984, bitterness toward Japan among trade officials and congressional representatives had reached truly worrisome levels.

This description of the Japanese policy behavior sounds very negative, but it should be tempered somewhat. All nations put the interests of domestic producers ahead of imports; Japan is not unusual and stands out primarily because of its rapid rise to the status of a major industrial exporter. At least the Japanese policy response has been in the correct direction; import barriers have fallen in Japan and will continue to do so. The Reagan administration may complain that it has made little progress or that Japan remains a closed market, but over the past four years the administration has achieved rather impressive concessions from Japan.

To expect Japan to play a much stronger leadership role in maintaining the liberal trade regime by independently and voluntarily lowering trade barriers without intense foreign pressure is unrealistic. The real danger lies in the possibility that Japan will cease to be conciliatory enough in the face of foreign pressures to liberalize. At the present time, such a possibility appears rather small, but the younger generation of Japanese government officials now beginning to move into positions of authority are more self-confident and less willing to appease what they often view as unfair foreign criticism.

The second influence on trade policy emerging from the economic changes of the past decade works against liberalization and increases the danger that Japan will cease to be conciliatory. As Japan entered industrial maturity and economic growth slowed, it faced new problems of declining industries. Japan is commonly thought to be a country that has protected its leading industries and has actively followed a policy of moving economic resources out of declining industries. I doubt whether Japan ever really followed such a policy, since it protected virtually all industries in the early postwar period. Nevertheless, as trade barriers have fallen in general, Japan now appears to do more to protect declining or ailing industries rather than the newly emerging growth industries.

Simply to be faced with a set of declining industries has been a new and unpleasant development for Japan. The causes lie in both the rise in the relative cost of labor after the mid-1960s as a result of successful industrialization and growth, and in the large jump in energy costs during the 1970s. The rise in labor costs has made Japan uncompetitive in agriculture, textiles, shipbuilding, and other relatively labor-intensive industries. The rise in energy costs affected all nations, but Japan relied on oil from the Middle East for a larger share of its energy needs than did most other countries (and still does). Therefore, it became uncompetitive internationally in aluminum refining, electric furnace steel, synthetic fibers, chemical fertilizers, and other products that require either large amounts of energy in the production process or petroleum-based inputs.

Japanese industries are no different from those in other countries: they do not want to go out of business and consequently put pressure on the government for aid and protection. To its credit, the Japanese government recognized that many of these industries were in decline and followed a policy of encouraging and helping them to reduce capacity. However, strong pressures have built for import barriers as well, and those pressures will continue. For agriculture, international uncompetitiveness has brought stiff import barriers and intense lobbying from the farmers to keep them. All nations protect agriculture for complex political and social reasons, but Japan is the object of great criticism because of its overall trade surpluses. Japan, therefore, faces a serious policy dilemma of how to deal with the domestic pressures for protection from uncompetitive industries in the face of strong international demands to lower import barriers. This is a question of particular interest to developing countries, since they are the efficient suppliers of labor-intensive products.

The serious policy question facing the Asian-Pacific region is whether these countries could or would absorb a larger share of Japanese exports if the United States were either to raise protectionist barriers against Japan or alter macroeconomic policy in such a way as to cause the dollar to fall in value against the yen, making the United States a less lucrative export market. Either scenario is a possibility. The bitterness toward Japan over trade issues could easily fuel a protectionist backlash against Japan. Concern is also rising in the United States over U.S. budget deficits, but if they are brought under control, then interest rates ought to fall, bringing down the dollar. This decline would mean that the United States would absorb less capital from abroad. Should either scenario come to pass, Japanese companies would be faced with higher prices for their products in the United States, leading them to redirect their export efforts to other parts of the world. As the most rapidly growing region of the world, with a number of industrializing countries seeking the kind of manufactured goods in which Japan excels, the Asian-Pacific region will be affected by any Japanese effort at export diversion.

But is this a realistic outcome? Two recent episodes suggest that Japanese exports are not always welcome in the region: a few years ago Taiwan banned the importation of some 1,500 items from Japan because of concern over its bilateral trade imbalance and frustration with Japanese trade barriers; and in 1984 South Korea followed the same path, banning 1,203 items. I have no answer to the question of whether the Asian countries would absorb considerably larger exports from Japan, but these two examples suggest that the redirection of Japanese exports toward Asia could become a very serious problem. The reaction of the region will depend heavily on whether perceptions of Japan as a protectionist country change.

Excerpt from the paper by Mao Yushi

THE UNITED STATES conducts an enormous amount of trade with nearly all the Asian-Pacific countries and regions. This tendency receives close attention from these countries and regions insofar as their economies depend heavily on foreign trade, particularly on trade with the United States.

At the end of World War II, the United States emerged as the world's biggest power. It produced nearly half of the world's total output, enjoyed one-third of world trade, and held three-fourths of the world's gold reserve in the early postwar years. In the subsequent thirty years, however, Germany, Japan, and the East Asian and ASEAN countries and regions gradually caught up while the United States was busy with its wars in Korea and Vietnam. The collapse of the Bretton Woods system in 1973 marked the close of the era when the United States dominated the whole world. At the start of the 1980s, the United States found itself mired in the longest recession since World War II. But the U.S. economy recovered quickly and has grown more rapidly than expected in the past two years. The growth of its GNP reached 6.9 percent in 1984, the fourth highest increase since World War II. For the first time in many years, U.S. economic growth exceeded Japan's. The recovery of the U.S. economy has pushed forward the world economy by absorbing imports from the other countries and regions.

Besides the accelerated growth of the U.S. economy in recent years, its two-digit inflation rate has been reduced to less than 4 percent and its unemployment rate to 7 percent. The stagflation that has troubled the U.S. economy for almost a whole decade seems to have been greatly alleviated.

The guidelines for coping with stagflation have not been furnished by any single school—Keynesianism, monetarism, or suppy side economics. Supply side economics has helped to improve U.S. economic efficiency by means of tax reduction and deregulation. Tax reduction has stimulated investment and consumption, albeit at the expense of a bigger deficit. Deregulation has promoted the reallocation of resources and has encouraged greater competition. The U.S. success in energy price deregulation has spurred the more efficient use of energy. Deregulation in aviation, railway, and some other public utility sectors has also yielded satisfactory results. These measures have promoted a more flexible economic structure, making it possible to readjust the allocation of resources to suit the changes in technology and preference. But the reduction in marginal tax rates makes the rich richer, and merciless competition makes the weak weaker. Such a policy, therefore, widens the gap between the rich and the poor and induces a social instability. It seems that there is no policy capable of eliminating this contradiction between equity and efficiency, and thus the U.S. economy will limp along as before.

Accordingly, the recovery of the American economy in 1984 does not mean the end of periodic recessions. Rather a much-discussed current topic is when the next recession will occur. Among the different views on the future of the U.S. economy, that of the U.S. government is the most optimistic. It predicts a bright future, mainly owing to the high value of the U.S. dollar. Exponents of this view find support for their theory—that capital flows, not trade flows, determine exchange market dynamics—in the fact that there is simultaneously a high U.S. dollar and a large deficit in the current account. Large amounts of capital flow to the United States, they insist, owing to favorable investment prospects and a healthy U.S. economy. They maintain that political stability, low taxes, high profits, and encouraging market opportunities are causes of this capital influx and, furthermore, suggest a bright future for the U.S. economy in the long run.

It is universally known, however, that commercial investment aims at profit, and the flow of profit back to foreign investors hinges on the international payment capability of the host country. In the long run, such capability can be achieved only by the export of commodities and services. If the current account of the United States continues to worsen, foreign investors may begin to doubt the United States' capability of international payment and withdraw their money, creating a ruinous situation for the U.S. money market and perhaps even seriously upsetting the world money market as a whole. Therefore, exclusive reliance on the influx of foreign capital in the absence of a healthy current account situation implies a great danger. Such a danger arises because individual investors are concerned only with investment returns to the neglect of macroeconomic imbalance.

The large flow of capital to the United States has given rise to friction among the developed countries. Owing to the outflow of capital to the United States, the European countries and Japan are short of funds for capital replacement. In the European countries, in particular, the current economic stagnation and decline in competitiveness in foreign trade are closely related to insufficient domestic investment. Understandably, the British government has seriously criticized the high-dollar policy of the United States. Banks on the Continent and in Britain have taken concerted action to reduce the value of the dollar. Although Japanese commodities are competitive, their competitiveness may suffer from insufficient capital replacement.

The high U.S. dollar adds to the burden of the developing countries, especially those deep in debt, and makes it more difficult for them to service their foreign debts. On the other hand, a policy that aims to boost the U.S. economy by shifting financial difficulties to the debtor nations implies danger for the United States. By 1983 loans extended by American banks to the developing countries had reached $130 billion, and the loans to Brazil, Mexico, and Venezuela from ten big U.S. banks had exceeded their combined assets. Breaking any link in the credit chain because of an inability to repay foreign loans may be destructive to all parties.

High interest rates combined with a high dollar may also reduce investment in the non-high-tech sectors of U.S. industry, because when the expected profit rate is lower than the interest rate, investors will quit the scene. Traditional U.S. industries are in need of equipment renewal, but the lack of funds makes this difficult. To encourage the investor, the U.S. government has introduced what are called investment tax credits, but this device is at the price of misallocation of resources.

The high dollar serves to reduce U.S. exports. The value of the dollar in early 1985 was 45 percent higher than it was four years ago, and it is estimated that such an appreciation has added $55 billion to the trade deficit each year. This alone has caused U.S. commodities to be less competitive, put many firms in unenviable conditions, and rendered 2 million people jobless. The U.S. government and its critics both have shown great concern over these phenomena. Unless checked in time, the high value of the dollar will increase the likelihood of protectionism, in which case the ensuing trade war will be highly costly to the whole world economy.

Of course, a strong dollar is not exceptionally disadvantageous to the U.S. economy. Nevertheless, from the preceding analysis one can see that, in contrast to the rosy picture painted by some people, a high dollar resulting from apparent prosperity contains a hidden danger. In fact, many American economists hope that the U.S. dollar will depreciate slowly so that there might be enough time for the U.S. economy to readjust to the new situation. However, the exchange market is something no one can manipulate, much as he might wish to.

Excerpt from the paper by Robert Z. Lawrence

THE U.S. budget deficit has indeed dominated the discussion of economic policy both domestically and abroad. Controversy over the implications of the deficit for the future course of the U.S. and world economies has marked the discussion. Much of the confusion results from a failure to recognize that the deficit has had both benefits and costs.

First, the particular combination of policy—extreme fiscal stimulus offset by monetary restraint—has produced substantial short-term benefits to the United States by achieving the major policy objective of recent years: a reduced rate of inflation. The fiscal stimulus—tax cuts for both consumers and businesses and a large defense buildup on the expenditure side—has been a big factor behind the strong recovery of domestic demand, production, and employment from the recession. At the same time, tight control over the supply of credit in the face of heavy government borrowing forced up U.S. interest rates and contributed to the inflow of foreign capital. The result was a tremendous rise in the foreign-exchange value of the dollar—totaling more than 50 percent since 1980. That rise in the value of the dollar, and the associated fall in import prices, contributed significantly to the decline in overall inflation. Several studies have found that roughly half of the reduction in inflation can be attributed to lower import prices. Thus the specific mix of policies allowed the United States to achieve a lower inflation rate at less cost to the domestic economy than if it had relied on domestic restraint alone.

Of course, the United States can be accused of following a beggar-thy-neighbor policy because the rising value of the dollar, while reducing inflation here, increased inflationary pressures in other countries. In addition, the heavy reliance on monetary restraint forced up interest rates and greatly intensified the debt-financing problems of developing nations, particularly in Latin America.

The ease with which the United States has been able to borrow overseas has been a major surprise to most American economists. Several years ago the standard forecast was that continued government borrowing at present magnitudes would initiate heightened competition for credit in the United States, raising interest rates and depressing investment. That forecast was wrong. Although sharply higher government deficits did lower the national saving rate, the offsetting rise in net foreign capital inflows has enabled the United States to maintain domestic investment at rates close to historical levels (table 1).

In prior years other countries—particularly in Europe—expressed great dissatisfaction with U.S. economic policy because of the strong inflationary pressures that the rise in the exchange rate placed on their economies. In addition, high interest rates in the United States inhibited their efforts to use monetary policy to stimulate their own economies. Attempts to lower interest rates led to an immediate outflow of capital to the United States and a fall in their exchange rate—exacerbating inflation. More recently, however, recognition has increased that the large trade deficit of the United States has been an important stimulus for the world economy. Increased exports to the United States have been the leading factor behind the limited economic recovery in Europe and are of enormous importance to Japan. Furthermore, the major economies of Latin America now have trade surpluses.

The sustainability of the high value of the dollar and the associated trade deficit have now become the major uncertainty in the U.S. economic outlook. If the United States should suddenly lose the capital inflow and be forced to live within its means, the low level of national saving would require a drastic curtailment of domestic investment. This situation could generate much higher interest rates in the United States and severe pressures on the financial market. Yet repeated forecasts that the dollar would decline or that foreigners would not continue to invest in the United States have so far proved wrong. The current situation has proved more sustainable than anticipated. In part, the contrasting circumstances of the United States and other industrial countries can explain this result. While the United States is short of saving, the rest of the industrialized world has been plagued by an excess of private saving relative to domestic investment. The export of that surplus to the United States has provided an important means of propping up economic activity in the rest of the world.

Table 1. *Saving and Investment as a Share of National Product, United States, 1951–84*

Saving and investment	Percent of net national product			
	1951–60	*1961–70*	*1971–80*	*1984*
Net savings[a]				
Private saving	8.4	9.2	8.9	9.4
Government saving	−0.7	−1.0	−2.0	−5.0
National saving and investment	7.7	8.2	6.9	4.4
Net foreign investment	0.3	0.6	0.0	−2.8
Private domestic investment	7.4	7.6	6.9	7.2

Source: Calculated by author with data from U.S. Department of Commerce, *National Income and Product Accounts of the United States, 1929–74,* and subsequent updates. See also *Survey of Current Business,* various issues.
a. Net saving and investment equals the gross flow minus capital consumption allowances (the depreciation of existing capital). Net national product equals gross national product minus capital consumption allowance. Pension funds of state and local governments are allocated to the private sector.

In several respects, the present situation is not dissimilar to that following the rise in oil prices in the mid-1970s. The accumulation of large trade surpluses (increased saving) by the OPEC countries focused concern on the need to recycle those funds. The recycling occurred when the OPEC countries deposited the surplus in U.S. banks, who in turn loaned the funds for investment in Latin America. A similar process was at work with the increased lending to the Eastern European countries. Today, the United States is playing the role of a large, less-developed country—importing capital. However, the United States has used the funds to support its own consumption—both public and private.

Some of the potential adjustment problems for the world economy are illustrated by considering the response to a reversal of the present U.S. economic policy. A substantial reduction in the budget deficit would eliminate much of the rationale for the current large trade deficit. Some offset would occur as lower interest rates promoted additional investment in the United States and abroad. However, it is difficult to believe that lower U.S. interest rates would add to domestic investment in Europe and Japan more than those countries would lose in exports to the United States. Even with lower interest rates, Latin America and other developing economies could not be expected to revert to the status of capital-importing countries in the near future.

Here in the United States there is a general belief that an easing of monetary policy could offset the depressive effects of a shift in fiscal policy toward restraint. Much of the presumed adjustment, however, relies on a fall in the value of the dollar and thereby a smaller trade deficit. If other countries resist such a loss of their export surplus, the adjustment could be more difficult than believed.

If the United States should find the political will to correct its budget deficit, prospects for long-term growth in the United States will depend on two other aspects of the economy, one favorable and one unfavorable. On the favorable side, the internal structure of the economy seems to be broadly satisfactory in its ability to adapt to changes in markets and technology. Compared with other industrial countries, American labor markets are relatively flexible and capable of adjusting to changes in the economic environment. On the dark side, however, the trend of productivity growth in the United States during the past decade has been significantly lower than during the postwar period, and the most competent economic research has yet to determine the principal causes of this situation.

Comments AMERICAN PARTICIPANT. One difference implicit in this discussion of American economic policy concerns its impact on the Pacific region. The imbalance in American policies leading to the expansion of the American economy has been remarkably positive for the countries of the Pacific Basin because it has been positive for Japan, creating a spillover effect. High interest rates and a strong dollar have increased the competitiveness of Japanese goods. Investment in fixed assets has become more lucrative for lenders because of high interest rates, and Japan is the major lender in the world. Acceptance by the United States of Japanese voluntary export restraints gave Japan a welfare windfall of $3 billion to $4 billion each year. Even in sectors where protectionism is high, this has not reduced trade, only slowed its growth.

The Pacific region criticizes American protectionism, but it also appreciates the United States as an engine of growth and recognizes that the United States is the most open of all the developed economies. Only Korea has been hurt by high interest rates. ASEAN has benefited from trade but has suffered a little from slightly lower commodity prices owing to the strong dollar. The real worry is about a slowdown in the American economy, because slow growth and protectionism in Japan and Europe make it nearly impossible for those markets to make up for a decline in American imports.

AMERICAN PARTICIPANT. The short-term effects of U.S. policy were high interest rates and the appreciation of the dollar. This caused debt burdens for other countries and an inflation of commodity and other prices. In the medium- to long-term, the strong dollar in turn stimulated exports so that the rest of the world began to see the benefits in increased growth. Over time, as these benefits have become visible, there has been increasing acceptance of American policies, not the increased isolation of the United States. If the American economy begins to slow, foreign countries may at first be grateful for the lower cost of the dollar, but later they may become concerned about the effect of the American recession on their own economic growth. But for now, the world has come to accept American policies, resulting in a lowering of tensions.

CHINESE PARTICIPANT. American economic policy is not stable. Policies to reduce the deficit and the rate of inflation have forced the government to issue bonds, effectively borrowing from foreign individuals and countries. It is fast becoming a debtor nation. According to the laws of economic development, after one or two years there will be another recession. After its advent, problems may reveal themselves that will have a bearing on the Asian–Pacific region.

AMERICAN PARTICIPANT. The Chinese appear to be more critical of the impact of American economic policies on Asia, while the Americans here stress the benefits. Even the Americans who criticize U.S. insensitivity to the third world feel that this evaluation is least applicable to Asia, and they usually feel it applies more to Latin America or Africa.

CHINESE PARTICIPANT. One serious readjustment in the American economy has been the expansion of service industries. More than 70 percent of the American labor force is employed in the service sector today, compared with only 50 percent in the 1950s. There are two subsectors of the service sector: one produces utility directly (restaurants, hotels, health care); the other provides services to other industries (insurance, communications, data processing and transmission). As the foreign market has grown, so have the risks and the need for more perfect information. Accordingly, risk has replaced transportation as the major element of transaction costs. The second subsector helps lower the risk. Trade improves efficiency, but trade has its own costs: insurance, transportation, information. If these costs are higher than the gains from efficiency, there will be a net loss, so there is an optimal level of trade.

The U.S. trade with Asia is larger than its trade with Europe, and American investments in Asia enjoy a higher rate of profit than those in Europe, suggesting that there should be more investment in Asia than is currently the case. But American uncertainties about the Asian market are also larger, owing to historical factors and differences in cultural background. Lowering the uncertainties through increased information will therefore lower the cost of trade, thereby increasing the volume of trade, which benefits both sides.

Excerpt from the paper by Mao Yushi

THE SHARE OF foreign trade in U.S. GNP grew from 6 percent in 1970 to 12 percent in 1984, about one-third of which was related to the Asian-Pacific region. U.S. foreign trade with this region, though limited, is important for both sides. The Asian-Pacific region is the largest consumer of American farm products, absorbing one-third of U.S. agricultural production. In the other direction, 90 percent of natural rubber consumed by the United States comes from Southeast Asia. By 1981 Indonesia had replaced Saudi Arabia as the United States' largest supplier of oil. Since 1975, two-way trade between the United States and Asia has surpassed that with Europe, and the difference has increased each year except in 1979. Trade with the Asian region overall has risen to one-third of the total foreign trade volume of the United States, even though in 1970 only 24 percent of U.S. imports were from the region and 23 percent of U.S. exports flowed in that direction. The Asian-Pacific region has become the biggest trade partner of the United States.

We can identify three categories in the trade between the United States and the Asian-Pacific economies. The first category of trade, including oil, rubber, and farm products, is attributable to differences in natural resources and is of a very stable character. The second category owes itself to differences in the level of economic development and thereby aids the structural change in the American economy. The United States imports labor-intensive goods from Asia to save labor for high-tech industries and then exports some of the output back to Asia, creating a complementary relationship. Since this picture may change because of the development of the LDCs, however, it is not as stable as the trade of the first category. The third category is trade in manufactured goods among the developed countries with different levels of technology and management. It is highly competitive and is liable to change with large inputs of capital and intelligence in a short period. A bundle of trade items between the United States and Japan belongs to that category.

The three categories of trade just described produce entirely different effects on the U.S. economy. From 1970 onward, large amounts of labor have been needed to develop the high-tech industries. It is estimated that most of the 26 million new jobs between 1970 and 1984 were absorbed by such industries. At the same time, the tertiary industries, including insurance, consultancy, forecasting, communications, data processing, and other services, have experienced a big boom. Because most of these services cannot be imported and can only be provided domestically, the U.S. economy has to save labor in other sectors to meet such a great demand for labor. Of course, these readjustments have not been without difficulties. Rather it has been a painstaking process, as thousands of people have had to leave their already familiar professions and environments, receive new training, and start over again at their new posts. This explains the wide support enjoyed by protectionism in the United States. From a macroeconomic perspective and over the long run, however, such structural change is justified, for otherwise there would not be such high labor productivity as there is now.

On the other side of the picture, trade among the developed countries is of a competitive rather than complementary character. The automobile trade between the United States and Japan is an excellent example. During the 1950s and 1960s, the United States exported a large number of cars to Japan, while in recent years Japanese cars have flooded the American market, numbering nearly 2 million a year since 1980. In recent years, U.S. car production reached its highest level since 1973, wresting back a sizable chunk of the market. The future is hard to predict. To prevail in the seesaw battle, both sides stake ever bigger inputs of capital, which may lead to a surplus of equipment in the car industry and a premature withdrawal of equipment from production. Such competitive trade between the United States and Japan also exists in audio-video equipment, semiconductor chips, office machines, and so forth. This is also true of the U.S.-European trade, especially in airplanes, communications equipment, nuclear power sets, and so forth. It is hard to say whether the structural readjustment of the U.S. economy will have positive or negative effects on such competitive exchanges.

Closer economic relations between the United States and the Pacific Basin have brought about corresponding changes in the U.S. economy. For example, the average per capita income in the five states along the Pacific ranks first among all regions of the United States. The westward movement of the population center has attained a speed of ten kilometers each year as against that of three kilometers each year earlier this century. This rate was reached only once before in the late nineteenth century, and the westward shift of the U.S. economic center is still continuing. Through the gradual changes within itself and in its surrounding environment, the United States has realized what the Pacific Basin means to it; it has come to the conclusion that closer relations with the Pacific make for more prosperous conditions worldwide.

Comments

CHINESE PARTICIPANT. I disagree with the view that the United States is shifting its priorities toward the Pacific. This judgment is premature. As I understand it, the strategic focus of the United States is still the Soviet-American relationship, which is focused in Europe and will remain there for some time. Undeniably, the economic position of the Pacific region is more and more important, but the focus of U.S. policy has not shifted. Trade volume alone is an incomplete measure of a shift in U.S. policy.

CHINESE PARTICIPANT. I share the view of a U.S. shift to the Pacific region. All available statistical data agree. In 1978 trade with the Pacific Basin exceeded trade with Europe by 24 percent. The same is true for U.S. foreign investment: in 1978–83 it grew by 65 percent in the Pacific region, but by only 3 percent in the aggregate. The shift toward the Pacific is especially true for the western states. In addition, the focus of the American economy is also shifting westward: a high percentage of resource production and modern manufacturing is now located in the west. The shift of the economic focus to the western United States and to the Pacific is comparable in importance to the shift toward the service sector in the overall structure of the economy.

CHINESE PARTICIPANT. Moreover, the United States is not paying enough attention to the Pacific region. Protectionism and embargoes on the export of high technology are examples of policies that are not conducive to trade with Asia. But the vast market and potential for investment make this region important. Europe pays more attention to the region than does the United States and is developing its relations there in a big way. In a long-term view, Europe has begun a real shift. The U.S. shift is too slow, much less than is there for Europe.

AMERICAN PARTICIPANT. I believe that U.S. trade policy is excessively concerned with bilateral trade imbalances in the Pacific Basin trade to the neglect of worldwide, multilateral issues. It is an unhealthy trend.

AMERICAN PARTICIPANT. This discussion of the relative importance of Europe and Asia agrees on the facts but not on how best to interpret them. In absolute terms, Europe is still more important to the United States than is East Asia, but in dynamic terms, the Asian-Pacific region has been narrowing the gap. Even though the political and military struggle with the Soviets is focused on

Europe, the Soviet military buildup in East Asia over the last ten to twenty years far exceeds the buildup in Europe and has forced the United States to shift its attention to determining how to maintain a balance of forces in the northwest Pacific. American investment in the Common Market countries is still much greater, but the future favors the Pacific. If the United States were to identify areas of vital interest, it would name both Europe and Asia, and possibly the Middle East, but could not specify which was the most important. I would like to draw your attention to a recent interview with [former] National Security Adviser Robert McFarlane in which he said that during Ronald Reagan's first term much attention was paid to building ties with Asia for both strategic and economic reasons, but that during Reagan's second term policymakers will devote more of their time and attention to Europe, particularly because of the perceived need to revitalize the Western European economies.[2]

North–South Relations and Protectionism

Excerpt from the paper by Gu Yuanyang

THE NORTH-SOUTH question is a global strategic problem. The North-South question in the Asian-Pacific region mainly manifests itself in the unequal economic relations between East Asia and Southeast Asia on the one hand and the developed countries on the other. The basic position of the nations of East Asia and Southeast Asia about the North-South question is somewhat different from that of other developing countries: they do not ask for much assistance from the countries of the North, but rather demand that they open their markets wider to exports from East Asia and Southeast Asia, increase investment in the region, and speed up technology transfer. These three basic issues will be the focus of North-South dialogue and cooperation in the Asian-Pacific region.

The deepening of North-South interdependence does not imply that the North-South relations in the Asian-Pacific region are harmonious. On the contrary, as the North-South economic relations have grown, the North-South contradictions have intensified, which are mainly reflected in the following aspects: One, the United States, Japan, and other developed countries have gained substantial control of manufacturing industries in the region

---

2. Leslie H. Gelb, "Taking Charge: The Rising Power of National Security Adviser Robert McFarlane," *New York Times Magazine* (May 26, 1985), p. 63.

through multinational corporations. This imposes a major constraint on the effort of the developing countries to develop their national industries. Two, the United States, Japan, and the other developed countries have controlled the export trade of this region through trading firms. Three, the developed countries are steadily expanding the marketing of their products, thus undermining local industries and deepening the economic dependence of the less developed countries. What is more, the developed nations control key technologies, and parts of many products cannot be resold to third countries without their consent. Four, the developed countries limit the import of "sensitive commodities" from this region by imposing voluntary export restrictions, quotas, and additional tariffs. Five, the United States, Japan, and other developed countries control the prices of international commodities through their raw material and energy reserves, thus affecting the interests of the exporting countries in the region.

It is obvious that unless the developed countries give serious consideration to the reasonable demands of the developing countries and forgo their policy of benefiting at the expense of others, it will be difficult for North–South cooperation in the Asian–Pacific region to achieve progress, and tension will inevitably occur in the North–South relations.

Excerpt from the paper by Wang Zengzhuang

IF THE economic-technical cooperation of the Asian-Pacific region is to be further strengthened, it is essential for the countries and areas concerned to adjust and improve their mutual economic relationships. It is particularly important to handle two kinds of relationships well. First, the North–South relationship. The developed countries should take practical steps to reduce and eliminate their protectionist measures in trade with the developing countries and areas, supply them with more soft loans and appropriate technologies, and help the debtor countries among them gradually to reduce their heavy debt burden. All this will serve their mutual interests. Next, the South–South relationship. The developing Asian-Pacific countries are a varied and dynamic group: they differ in their stage of development, their industrial structures are constantly changing, and some have already become exporters of capital and technology as a result of quick economic growth. Consequently, there are increasing opportunities for economic and technical cooperation among them. The progress made in intra-ASEAN cooperation is a case in point. Naturally, competition exists among developing countries, too, but they can regulate it through friendly consultations based on equality and mutual benefit so that it will not hamper cooperation.

Excerpt from the paper by Wang Dingyong

A SALIENT FEATURE of North-South trade relations in the Asian-Pacific region is the American and Japanese export of capital-intensive and technology-intensive products and their import of labor-intensive products from the developing countries. Because of trade conflicts between them, as well as the rise of oil prices and the new technological revolution, both the United States and Japan have shifted some of their labor-intensive industries to developing countries, thus spurring the growth of the textile industry, light industry, and assembly industry in developing countries and areas that have a large labor force. The United States and Japan export steel products, transport vehicles, factory equipment, intermediary products, and key parts to the newly industrialized areas and the ASEAN countries. And the United States and Japan import textiles, garments, electric household appliances, and other light consumer items from those regions. Therefore, North-South trade relations reflect both the existence of the irrational international division of labor and the competition among the developed countries for markets in developing countries and regions.

The competition between the United States and Japan in the rest of Asia stands out most conspicuously, as can be seen in their balances of trade. Although the United States exports technologies, equipment, and intermediary products to the newly industrialized areas and the ASEAN countries, it is still often plagued by a trade deficit. Japan, on the other hand, enjoys a surplus in trade with the newly industrialized areas and the ASEAN countries. One reason is that Japan imports fewer labor-intensive products from these countries and areas than does the United States. The major cause, however, is that the capital-intensive products of the United States are no match for the Japanese products, giving Japan a larger share of the market than the United States in these countries. As a result, the developing countries' balance of payment surplus with the United States is in contrast to their trade deficit with Japan. Until a fundamental change in the trade structure occurs, namely, before technology-intensive products become the focus of market competition between the United States and Japan, this trend is not likely to change.

Comments

CHINESE PARTICIPANT. North-South contradictions in the Asian-Pacific region are not as acute as in other regions, but the course of future developments will have a serious impact. Japanese concessions to the United States hurt the interests of the developing countries in the region, and their restrictions on imports of chickens and plywood anger Indonesia and Thailand. Although Japan's concessions do not amount to much, the tendency to make concessions to the United States and not to other countries is important. Japan is less forthcoming than the United States in technology transfer and investment; this feeling is shared by other countries in the region. The United States has recently proposed talks in the General Agreement on Tariffs and Trade on agriculture and the service sector. The Asian-Pacific region feels the United States is pursuing its own interests without giving attention to solving the problems of developing countries. Protectionism is also a problem: it is difficult for countries in the process of development to keep protectionism at a low level. Other problems about multinational corporations and restrictive business practices need solutions.

CHINESE PARTICIPANT. We should consider this question with a two-pronged approach: first, economic and political relations between the United States and East and Southeast Asia are strengthening; and, second, with the strengthening of such ties, competition and contradictions are arising.

Since 1975, ASEAN has held ongoing talks with the United States, Japan, Australia, New Zealand, Canada, and the European Community (EC). The six-plus-five dialogue has been marked by struggles between the developed and the developing countries and has not produced the results that have been anticipated. The ASEAN countries have even said that they would give up the dialogue if it does not produce greater benefits. It is doubted that they will carry through on this threat, but in saying so they are warning that North-South contradictions exist. Indeed there has been no real progress in North-South relations since the Paris meeting of 1975.

Excerpt from the paper by He Fang

THE NORTH-SOUTH question is becoming more and more complicated and acute because the developing nations are confronted with serious economic difficulties. After World War II, the developing nations enjoyed great success in developing their national economies. However, since the beginning of the 1980s they have been severely hit by the economic crisis in the capitalist world. Their rate of development has suddenly decreased, and there has been universal deterioration in their economic situation. Of course, the levels of their economic development vary greatly. But as far as most of them are concerned, they will be in great difficulty throughout the 1980s.

A new technological revolution is in the making. On the one hand, it adds new ingredients to the traditional division of labor and accelerates the progress of the internationalization of economic life; on the other, it injects new complicating elements into the relations between the developed nations and those between the South and the North, thus making the contradictions among them even more acute. To the developed nations, whoever is in the lead in technology may well be superior in economic level and competitiveness. Therefore, since the beginning of the 1980s, an important element of the increased competition among the United States, Japan, and the European countries has been to research, develop, and apply sophisticated technology. Such competition is turning white hot day by day. These countries are, in the meantime, monopolizing the results of the technological revolution and discriminating against the developing nations, thus widening the economic gap between the South and the North.

The developed nations, the United States in particular, insist on a rigid attitude on the North-South question, trying in every way to uphold the old international economic order so as to shift the crisis onto the developing nations and intensify their exploitation. For example, the developed countries force down the prices of raw materials and fuel, limit importation of manufactured goods from the developing nations, assume an unfair attitude in the transfer of technology and financial cooperation, and let the developing nations bear the heavy load of huge foreign debts and high interest rates. This makes the North-South conflict escalate continually in the direction of a fierce confrontation. Not long ago, West Germany's Chancellor Helmut Kohl predicted in a press interview that, by the end of this century or definitely by the beginning of the next one, the impact of North-South conflict would have exceeded the East-West conflict.

Japan is even more dependent on the developing nations. That is why its attitude toward the North-South question seems more flexible, but its words are more impressive than its deeds. Given the fact that Japan's trade friction with the developed nations is increasing with each passing day, expanding its economic cooperation with the developing nations should be an important way out for Japan. The Japanese government has time and again resolved to encourage direct investment in the developing nations and to increase its economic aid. What hampers the quick progress of economic cooperation with the developing nations is the fact that high American interest rates have attracted tremendous amounts of Japan's surplus capital. However, as the situation changes, Japan will gradually strengthen its activities in the developing countries.

Excerpt from the paper by Wang Dingyong

THE INTENSIFYING trade protectionism will adversely affect trade in the Asian-Pacific region, and particularly the trade in labor-intensive products. The United States and other technologically developed capitalist countries mainly export machinery, transport vehicles, and basic materials. To change the structure of their economies, improve their technological levels, and develop their industries, developing countries normally do not impose restrictions on the import of technology and machinery from the developed countries. Therefore, trade protectionism comes mainly from the United States and other developed countries. In particular, restrictions imposed by them on imports of both labor-intensive products of traditional industries (such as fiber products, shoes, and leather products) and labor-intensive products of new industries (such as electric household appliances) directly affect the export trade of developing countries.

The serious barriers to trade caused by trade protectionism will intensify contradictions and difficulties in the world economy and international economic relations. Protectionism not only impairs the interests of developing countries, but will also bring adverse effects to the economic recovery of the developed countries. In particular, trade within the Asian-Pacific region absorbs more than half of the total export of all countries in the region. With their rapidly growing economies and expanding markets, the developing countries and areas in this region have become important trade partners of the United States, Japan, and other developed countries. Hence trade protectionism of the developed countries will inevitably affect the economic development of the ASEAN countries and the newly industrialized areas, leading to reductions of their imports, particularly of machinery equipment, steel products, various intermediary products, and key parts from the developed countries. Therefore, trade protectionism hurts those who practice it as well as those at whom it is directed.

Competition and cooperation among developing countries and areas in the Asian-Pacific region will be an important trend in the trade development of this region. Owing to restrictions imposed by trade protectionism, these countries and areas will naturally face increasingly sharp competition in their export of labor-intensive products. At present, China's exports consist mainly of labor-intensive products, such as textiles, garments, leather products, toys, sporting goods, articles of daily use, daily pottery ware, processed food, cosmetics, tourist commodities, shoes, furniture, handicraft articles, electric household appliances, and so forth. The export of these products will compete with the same products from ASEAN and the newly industrialized areas. Because the developing countries and areas are close in their level of economic development, competition among their products on the world market will urge them constantly to improve the quality of their products and to increase varieties, thus accelerating the transformation of their industrial structures. Meanwhile, this competition will enable them to bring into full play their own advantages, strengthen cooperation among them, and promote a balanced division of labor among them. What is more important, since there is a huge potential for growth in their domestic markets, as long as there is competition in export, their economic development will also lead to an increase in imports. Therefore, one should not only see competition; one will also see mutual assistance, strengthened division of labor, and cooperation.

Comments

AMERICAN PARTICIPANT. Footwear is a classic example of the attempts of developed countries to protect their domestic industries from labor-intensive imports. I have looked at the influence of orderly marketing arrangements with Taiwan and South Korea on the shoe trade and discovered that for a time U.S. employment increased, the market share of imports from Taiwan and South Korea decreased, and other Asian exporters enjoyed an increased market share.[3] These were the expected results of import restrictions, but they were not long lasting. When the arrangements were removed, imports increased to make up for their earlier stagnation, and Taiwan and South Korea squeezed out competitors. To the extent that American firms adjusted, they did so by shifting production abroad, specializing in higher value-added merchandise, and engaging in some technological innovation.

My conclusions were the following: first, orderly marketing arrangements have no effect on a declining industry. Second, protectionism has not prevented imports from gaining a substantial market share. Imports have still done very well, although not as well as without protectionist policies. Third, the type of protectionism matters. Orderly marketing arrangements are selective discrimination against particular countries and are inefficient. If we choose to protect an industry, we must do so in an efficient way.

A more sophisticated definition and analysis of protectionism is needed. Although protectionism does exist in the United States,

---

3. Orderly marketing arrangements are bilateral or multilateral agreements that specify the volume or value of trade to be conducted in particular commodities.

there is still much access to the American market. The Chinese need to understand and influence U.S. trade policy by testifying, lobbying, and retaliating against unilateral action by the United States, as in the case of textiles. China should not simply complain once the decision is made.

AMERICAN PARTICIPANT. Protectionism is not a problem for commodity exports from Southeast Asia, only for manufactured exports. The evidence is that high commodity prices created several problems for those countries that rely on commodity exports. One problem is an inflated exchange rate that constricts exports of all goods except that one commodity. Another is that these governments do not know how to use the money earned through exports. The result is mismanagement of domestic resources, corruption, and waste.

The goals of protectionism are first, to maintain welfare, employment, or political support; second, to ensure national security; and third, to protect infant industries. The last one is the only argument that promotes growth; the first two cause slower growth. But all economists agree that a country may need to protect certain industries for its security.

CHINESE PARTICIPANT. The demands of the third world for a new international economic order should be reasonable. Excessive demands will not lead to good relations between North and South, which should be the point of the process. Both sides—North and South—have to make concessions. Issues such as the country-of-origin question should be resolved through global, regional, or bilateral negotiations, not through confrontation.[4]

North-South relations in the Asian-Pacific region are improving but problems persist. The demand of the countries in the region is for the West to open its markets, increase investments in the region, and increase the pace of technology transfer. The developed countries must continue to make concessions to improve North-South cooperation.

AMERICAN PARTICIPANT. The suggestion was made that developed countries must make more concessions. But I believe that the developed countries should be tougher in negotiations with the developing countries and should demand open markets in

4. In August 1984 the Reagan administration announced changes in the regulations governing textile imports. Goods originating in one country (for example, China) that underwent final processing in another country (for example, Hong Kong) before being shipped to the United States would thereafter be counted under the import quota of the first country rather than the second. The result of the rule was to tighten the limits on Chinese textile imports to the United States.

return for concessions. Even though the Asian LDCs are experiencing high rates of growth in their economies and in trade, these rates are inhibited by their own trade restrictions. The protectionism of the developing countries hurts other developing countries the most, since it is South-South trade that has been increasing faster than any other type of world trade. Not one of the Asian-Pacific countries has fully opened its markets to trade, whether to developed countries, developing countries, or even other NICs. We need to reintroduce the concept of reciprocity.

Protectionism does not increase resources, it only rearranges how one uses them. Protectionism is not necessary for development: Hong Kong is an example of successful development without protectionism.

CHINESE PARTICIPANT. Hong Kong cannot be cited as an example for China because Hong Kong is a free port that relies on commerce, finance, and transshipment to promote certain light industries, mainly in the assembly sector. Japan is a more typical example of how countries modernize through the use of protectionist policies.

CHINESE PARTICIPANT. It is true that protectionism does not create value or resources, but it is still necessary for industrial development. The United States and Japan both had strong protectionist policies during their development. Japan controlled foreign exchange by importing only necessary goods.

CHINESE PARTICIPANT. Your demand for reciprocity in the opening of markets brings up an important question. The United States wants to open agricultural trade and put farm products, investment, and services under the GATT, but the developing countries disagree. In the Asian-Pacific region, some countries may agree with some of these ideas, but the third world as a whole disagrees. Can most of the third world countries agree with this proposal of the United States? If the third world will not support the American proposal, what will the United States do next? If the third world does not accede to American demands in the GATT for lower barriers to trade in agriculture and services, then Washington has threatened to create more special relationships—like the new common market with Israel—to favor those trading partners who are more accommodating.

AMERICAN PARTICIPANT. That comment does not capture the American position on the GATT. First, the United States wants to restore the GATT as the central institution in trade rather than to abandon it. One aspect of this aim is to develop the GATT's ability to solve trade problems that are outside current GATT rules. The Asian-Pacific countries have a stake here in finding ways of regulating orderly marketing arrangements and other restrictions. Another issue is the use of subsidies to promote exports to gain market shares beyond some legitimate level. Particularly in agriculture, which is entering an era of new technology, we need to let countries with a comparative advantage capture markets, not the richest countries who can afford the subsidies. A third issue is the need to find a way of enforcing GATT rules now in existence. The rules of the GATT require unanimous agreement before action can be taken, meaning that even the countries in violation must agree first. Together, these issues constitute the main priority of the United States.

Beyond these considerations, a second range of priorities affects the new issues of high technology, services, and investment. A third is the introduction of trade liberalization measures on a global scale. Thus the U.S. position on new GATT negotiations is not limited only to services or investment, although these are the issues that have received the most attention.

AMERICAN PARTICIPANT. It was a mistake for the Tokyo Round to create separate levels of treatment in the GATT for developed and developing countries. This action created a kind of double standard in international economics, in which developing countries were treated more favorably than developed countries. The decision weakened the constituency for liberalization in the United States. In addition, the fact that developing countries are exempted from GATT provisions means that the GATT now deals principally with issues of interest to the developed countries. For example, it took ten years to negotiate the Generalized System of Preferences for the developing countries in the GATT, and this program is actually rather stingy. Although the GATT agenda is now set by the developed countries, the developing countries could refocus the agenda if they would be willing to make some concessions.

AMERICAN PARTICIPANT. I agree that it would be unwise to discuss trade in a North-South context. For one thing, there has never been a strong political constituency in this country for foreign aid or for other forms of assistance to the developing countries. Moreover, defining the issues in North-South terms overlooks the enormous diversity within each of the two blocs. Singapore and the Asian NICs cannot be lumped together with Africa; and the Europeans do not go along with the United States on economic issues. In the Law of the Sea negotiations, for example, Europe gave concessions that the United States refused to accept.

CHINESE PARTICIPANT. Developing countries get the short end of trade negotiations. Inequality in the levels of development among countries has carried over from history and is now taken for granted. The challenge is to replace the existing inequality with equality and mutual benefit, because the present situation benefits neither the developed nor the developing countries.

CHINESE PARTICIPANT. The developing countries are now in the process of industrialization and want to adopt appropriate measures to protect their national industries and their trade. Such policies are an objective and natural requirement in the process of development.

In contrast, protectionism in the developed countries does not help either side. It reduces imports of advanced goods and technology by developing countries, slowing their development and limiting the growth in world trade. The U.S. policy on textiles hinders exports from the developing countries, who therefore cannot buy more from the United States. When China's exports decrease as a result of the country-of-origin rule, for example, it cannot buy more machinery from the United States. If the exports of developing countries are restricted, their industrialization will be slowed. This result is not beneficial either to the developing countries or to the United States and other developed countries.

U.S. protectionism poses a threat to the developing countries in Asia because the United States is their largest trading partner. There is a mutual reliance in the Pacific region: changes in the American economy, exchange rates, and interest rates will have an impact on the region. The United States is not inclined toward lowering import restrictions but instead toward raising them.

AMERICAN PARTICIPANT. The concern in Asia over American protectionism is legitimate, but to imply that the United States is the most restrictive country is wrong. To suggest that the American markets are more closed to the manufactured exports of developing countries than is Japan defies any reasonable understanding of the situation.

How much regulation of trade is legitimate for any country? If, as some of our Chinese colleagues have suggested, the United States is in the midst of a new technological revolution, one could go on to describe the United States as a "newly developing industrialized country." By that definition it should be entitled to the same protectionism as is claimed by the developing countries of the third world. Third world countries claim the right to manage their economies and trade to guide economic development. If this is true for them, can it not be so for the United States to ensure the readjustment in the American economy that is necessary for new development?

CHINESE PARTICIPANT. Developing countries do impose restrictions on imports, sometimes more severely than do developed countries. But they protect fledgling industries, whereas the developed countries protect old and backward industries.

Many East Asian countries that have a trade surplus with the United States have a deficit with Japan, so for these countries trade with the United States compensates for the closed market in Japan. In the past, the American market was open, a protectionist trend is increasingly worrisome. This trend does not mean that protectionism in the United States is likely to become as serious as that in Japan, but it does warrant our attention. Moreover, if the United States succeeds in pressuring Japan to reduce exports to the United States, those exports will simply be channeled to other countries in the Asian-Pacific region, resulting in worse trade balances between them and Japan. Japan's refusal to open its markets will increase the objections to U.S. protectionism.

AMERICAN PARTICIPANT. In the early postwar period, the Japanese government erected very high trade barriers, including both strict quotas and high tariffs. Beginning in the early 1960s, the process of dismantling these barriers began and is still continuing. As a result of these changes, Japanese tariffs are now generally low, although certain individual goods, such as plywood, liquor, and certain foods, still have high duties. Quotas exist largely for agricultural goods or for manufactured goods closely related to agriculture, such as leather. The Japanese now accept the need for higher quotas for certain minor goods, but not for beef or citrus. There are other trade barriers in the form of stringent quality standards, including detailed inspection of each imported good when it arrives in Japan. The United States accepts Japanese certification of the fitness of its exports without inspection, but Japan insists on inspecting all imports.

There has been progress in increasing quotas and lowering standards, but not as much as we had hoped. Even so, Japan does import billions of dollars of goods, and its imports include manufactured goods as well as raw materials. Both aspects of this situation need to be kept in mind as we examine Japan's foreign trade account.

China's Reforms and the Future

THE REFORM of agricultural policy, industrial management, and the planning system that has been undertaken since 1978 and the "open economy" policy that seeks to attract foreign trade and technology are the two major aspects of the reform of the Chinese economy. Although both the American and Chinese delegations generally agreed about the nature and success of the reforms already in place, views differed over the potential difficulties in the next round of reforms and over the principal characteristics of China's economy once the reforms have run their course. Participants also disagreed about the types of foreign technology and investment that are appropriate to China's needs and about the prospects for dramatic increases in Sino-Japanese trade.

The Domestic Reforms

Excerpt from the paper by Robert F. Dernberger

CHINA's domestic economic reforms fall into three categories. Agricultural reform began with the rise to power of the Deng Xiaoping-Zhao Ziyang-Hu Yaobang leadership group in 1978 and already has become an important feature of China's economy, producing clear results in the statistics of economic performance. Reform of enterprise management has long been discussed and has been the subject of several experimental reforms. But only recently, as the specific objective of the urban industrial reform campaign adopted by the Third Plenum of the Party's Central Committee in October 1984, has reform begun in earnest. Thus, at the present time anyway, the available statistics for enterprise efficiency remain unimpressive. Beginning in 1985 the Chinese are introducing a serious attempt to reduce the scope of mandatory, centrally determined and administered plans. Despite the lack of proven results for the reform of both enterprise management and central planning, I do believe that in each area—agriculture, enterprise, planning—we can expect identifiable changes to become characteristic of China's new economy.

39

The most significant economic reform and the one most established as a long-term feature of China's economy was not even introduced as part of the leadership's reform program. The third plenum in 1978 adopted a policy of increasing the prices to be paid to agricultural producers and issued a revised version of the "Sixty Articles" on agriculture.[1] This document was an attempt to restore production and income distribution decisions to the basic level of the three-tiered collective organization in agriculture (the commune, the brigade, and the team) and assure the team that its obligations would be fixed and not changed at will by higher levels, nor would its resources be requisitioned without compensation. The document made no reference to the household responsibility system and later official statements made it clear that party authorities did not include household farming as part of their economic reform program. Once the Sixty Articles signaled a new period of relaxation of controls over agricultural production, however, local authorities and the peasants—protected by the party secretaries in Sichuan and Anhui—soon began to introduce their own reforms, creating a movement in the rural sector that higher-level authorities were unable to resist. In the end, the Chinese leadership accepted this dramatic change in the institutional organization of production and income distribution in agriculture and adopted it as the household responsibility system.

The major feature of the household responsibility system was the rejection of collectivization in favor of household farming. As originally introduced, of course, it did not replace the three-tier collective organizations. But the taxes, quota deliveries to the state, the welfare fund, and investment and operating charges of the collectives were divided up as individual household responsibilities. In return for their agreement to meet their share of these responsibilities, the contracting households were provided their share of the collective's land, the use of its machinery and equipment, and an allocation of such inputs as seeds and fertilizer. The household was then free to organize and carry out its own production activities, being allowed to keep any excess output produced beyond contract obligations. The household could consume this excess, sell it to the state at above-quota delivery prices, or sell it on the markets, which were reestablished in both the rural and urban areas.

1. This is a draft document called "Decisions of the Central Committee of the Chinese Communist Party—Some Questions Concerning the Acceleration of Agricultural Development."

The introduction of the household responsibility system was but the first step in a series of reforms that irresistibly unfolded to the point that market forces now largely determine production and income distribution in the agricultural sector in China. First of all, to encourage investment in the land, the household is guaranteed rights to the use of land for fifteen years or more. Second, to better adjust the amount of land used by the contracting household to its labor power, skills, and ambition, land can be reallocated by the households, subject to the approval of the collective. Not only can a household relinquish its right to land entirely and specialize in sideline, industrial, or other activities, but those who acquire more land because of their superior skills can also "hire" workers to work the land they have accumulated. In theory, there is little households cannot do in the way of producing goods and services if they have the skills and resources to do so. Equally important, they are encouraged to choose their production of goods and services on the basis of market possibilities so as to maximize their income.

Output and personal incomes in the agricultural sector have increased dramatically and explain much of the improvement in macroeconomic indicators for the entire Chinese economy during the past decade. With the increase in output, the state can obtain the deliveries it needs at market prices and avoid the need for allocating those quotas across the board in the manner that most taxes and delivery quotas are assigned in the socialist economies. As a result, the Chinese authorities are reintroducing the "advance purchase system" of the early 1950s, in which the purchasing agents of the state obtain promises from peasant producers to deliver a specified amount of output at harvest time in return for a guaranteed price and advance payment of a portion of the delivery price. With this change, Chinese agricultural production and income distribution will have returned to much the same system that existed in the early days of the collectivization movement in the mid-1950s. Moreover, to remove the inconsistencies between bureaucratic administration and household farming, the agricultural sector has been decollectivized. The townships have been reestablished, the communes are being dismantled, and the brigade remains the unit of administration and supervision as far as the collective is concerned, while the household has become the basic unit of production in Chinese agriculture once again.

Inefficiencies obviously are involved in the management and operation of the typical Chinese enterprise, and the impact of more than a decade of radical economic principles and policies has made conditions even worse. Thus reforms in enterprise management have been an objective of the economic reform program almost from the very beginning, and a wide variety of experiments have been introduced over the past several years. Before 1985, however, enterprise reforms were neither as sweeping nor as firmly in place as the reforms in the agricultural sector. The major reforms that did represent significant changes in enterprise management were in three areas: the management authority of the director, the organization of the enterprise, and the allocation of the enterprise's output or services.

The party was to withdraw from interfering in the day-to-day operations of the enterprise, and the director was to assume more identifiable individual responsibilities and authority in running the enterprise. Quite simply, the authorized decisions and assigned responsibilities of the enterprise management would be assumed by those individuals so identified in the enterprise's own organization chart, and those people were to be chosen on the basis of their education and technical skills. The whole purpose of this reform was the professionalization of enterprise managers and the routinization of their work, free from interference from government bureaucrats, party cadres, and the workers. Effectively implementing this reform, of course, is a lengthy and difficult problem. Although considerable progress has been made in certain industries and areas, the successful completion of this transition is far from certain and is unlikely to occur in the immediate future.

A second type of enterprise reform has taken place and is readily observable in China. The reform not only encourages the creation of collective and private enterprises to compete with or complement existing state enterprises, but also permits the leasing of state enterprises to collectives or individuals. This change represents an opening up of economic activities such as transport, trade, production, and especially services to nonstate enterprises to increase the variety of goods and services available. It also reduces those areas in which the state enterprises enjoy a monopoly and, thus, also creates more competitive forces to enrich the quality of existing commodities and services.

Finally, not only has enterprise reform changed the structure of enterprises to a mix of state, collective, and individual enterprises, but the allocation of the output of goods and services of those enterprises has also been reformed. The scope of commodities and services included in the plan and distributed by the state's unified system of trade has been reduced. Some commodities and services can be traded directly among units in a limited price range, and some commodities and services can be sold on a relatively free market. Quite simply, not only have the types of enterprises producing goods and services increased to include alternatives to the traditional state enterprises, but the ways for distributing goods and services have also been increased.

The third major reform in enterprise management that has been adopted as official policy by the party affects the distribution of the profits of the enterprise. The principle of revenue sharing by units of government and enterprises for incentive purposes was introduced very early in the current program of economic reform, but this principle did not introduce a major change in how the traditional state enterprise was managed in a Soviet-type economy. Yet the Chinese have recently decided to eliminate the practice of incorporating the profits and losses of a state enterprise in the state's budget as a revenue or as an expenditure, respectively. In the future, state enterprises will be responsible for their own profits and losses, that is, the residual after payment of the normal commodity and business taxes and a new tax on profits.

This reform was supposed to have been carried out by 1984, but it has been continually delayed because of the need to determine a special additional tax (or subsidy) that must be included in the transition period. As a result of the traditional economic system and its distorted price system, individual enterprises had operated with a wide range of profits and losses—even within the same industry. To make them suddenly responsible for their own profits and losses in order to stimulate efficient management would be most inequitable and would reward inefficient enterprises in profitable industries while penalizing efficient enterprises in un-profitable industries, with the rate of profitability being determined by irrational prices or exogenous forces. Thus for the period of transition to the new system, an "adjustment" tax must be determined for each enterprise. The principle to be used in determining this tax is to leave the enterprise with the same amount of retained earnings after the new system is introduced as it had retained in the previous year under the old system. Once the transition has been carried out, it is hoped that it will be possible to eliminate steadily the adjustment tax and place the enterprise in a position of trying to increase efficiency—cut costs, introduce technological innovations, improve product quality, and increase factor productivity—so as to increase its profits. The increased profits can be used to finance investment, the workers' welfare fund, and increased wages and bonuses for the workers.

If successful, of course, this reform would make the Chinese enterprise a very different type of enterprise than is typical in a Soviet-type economy, but the outcome will depend heavily on the results of the reform of the planning and price systems.

The need for price reform and reform of the planning system has been recognized and discussed ever since the economic reform program was introduced in 1978, but few concrete proposals have been developed and implemented so far. In all of the socialist, centrally planned economies, commodities and their prices have always been placed in three categories: commodities produced according to centrally determined, mandatory plans and sold by the producer at fixed prices; commodities produced according to administrative guidance and sold at negotiated prices; and commodities produced according to the decisions of the producing unit and sold on the market at market prices. The effects of China's reforms in planning and price determination have been evident over the past few years. Significantly, the Chinese have reduced the share of production and transactions carried out in the centrally planned sector and expanded the share of production and transactions in the noncentrally planned sector.

The document on urban industrial reform adopted by the Third Plenum of the Twelfth Central Committee in October of 1984 suggested an important change in the pace of transition from a centrally planned and controlled economy to one in which the central planners controlled only the "commanding heights." The same document indicated that the initial steps in a true price reform would be introduced in the near future. The document did not spell out the policies, strategies, and institutional changes that would constitute the reform of the planning system or the price system, but it did indicate that these reforms would be introduced in the next few years. The changes to be introduced in the system of planning are depicted in the oft-repeated claim that the role of mandatory planning will be reduced, while that of guidance planning and the market will be increased.

While we are familiar with the functioning of mandatory planning and the market, it is guidance planning that is likely to become the largest sector of the three. Therefore, the term requires some clarification if one hopes to describe China's future economic policies, strategies, and institutions. My own understanding of the term guidance planning is that it means the central planners will no longer set all the detailed microoutput and microinput targets that now make up the mandatory plan. Instead, they will allow lower authorities—ministries, provinces, municipalities, counties, and so forth—to control a greater proportion of inputs and outputs. In other words, certain quantities of steel products will still be governed by mandatory targets assigned by the central government to specific enterprises, which will be guaranteed supplies of inputs so they can meet their assigned output targets. Besides these mandatory plans for steel, additional steel output targets and a share of the necessary inputs will be distributed to lower levels of the economic and political administration. These aggregates, in turn, will be distributed to the enterprises in a process including negotiations between the lower levels of the political and economic administration and the enterprises they administer. These are the guidance plans. It is hoped that compliance with the guidance plans will be voluntary, not mandatory, and it is believed volunteers will be forthcoming because those who have the output targets to assign also control some of the necessary inputs and can guarantee delivery of those inputs.

In one sense, this policy of guidance planning replacing mandatory planning can be interpreted as a change to decentralized planning, but the reform of the planning system being introduced in China is more dramatic than the mere decentralization of the planning process. On the one hand, a particular commodity is no longer restricted to a single method for determining its output and distribution: a portion of the commodity's production will be carried out within the mandatory plan and assigned by the central authorities; a portion will be produced within the guidance plan negotiated and administered by lower-level authorities (although a ministry remains a fairly high level of authority); while a portion of the commodity's production will be carried out for sale on the market. On the other hand, an individual enterprise no longer belongs totally within a single sector; any enterprise—state, cooperative, or private—can produce output for all three sectors. For instance, defense industries are encouraged to produce motorcycles for private households. If ever the term "mixed system" was an appropriate description for an economy, it is for China's economy of the future. The implementation of this reform, however, has just begun, and the mandatory planned sector remains the dominant sector in the Chinese economy at present.

While it has been recognized that most other aspects of the economic reform require price reform, the discussions of price reform—at both the theoretical and applied level—are rather general and include such phrases as "This is a serious problem and requires study," or "We need to develop a specific solution or plan before we proceed," or "It will take a lengthy period to achieve a reform of our price system." I have not read, nor am I aware of, any concrete proposal for price reform in China. It is true, of course, that the document on urban industrial reform cited price reform as a major target, and that Zhao Ziyang's "Report on the Work of the Government" presented to the Third Session of the Sixth National People's Congress in 1985 cited wage and price reform as one of the major tasks in 1985. Yet neither document provides a specific program of price reform.

Two of the most successful aspects of China's economic reform program have been the rapid increase in agricultural production and peasant incomes and the increase in the standard of living of the population as a whole. The agricultural reforms will continue to spur output in the agricultural sector, but the pace of growth will be somewhat lower than it has been in the past few years. Much of the very rapid growth in the past few years has been because of one-time shifts in the production function: the increased incentives owing to the increase in prices for output and the creation of household farms as the decisionmaking unit in production and income distribution; the restoration of traditional cropping patterns, markets, and sideline activities; the initial stimulus to noncrop production activities—timber, fishing, animal husbandry, sericulture, and so forth; and several consecutive years of the best weather China has enjoyed for many decades. They will be sufficient, however, to allow for continued annual increases in incomes and the standard of living. Finally, the rate of growth will be high enough to continue the process of reducing China's dependence on imports of agricultural products, while simultaneously restoring China's traditional capacity as one of the world's great agricultural exporters.

The progress in the reforms in planning, industrial management and organization, and the price system I believe will be best characterized as "muddling through," that is, not nearly as successful as the reforms in agriculture. Nonetheless, most countries have learned how to achieve acceptable economic performance while maintaining economic policies, strategies, and institutions that may be charitably described as the result of muddling through. Furthermore, Chinese policies, strategies, and institutions in planning, enterprise management and organization, and the price system will in the foreseeable future represent a considerable improvement in comparison with the two decades before the death of Mao. In other words, I do not see China replicating the economic miracles of Japan or of the newly industrialized countries (NICs). Rather China's economic modernization will be achieved through a lengthy process of steady growth, as the implementation of the economic reforms steadily improves the nonquantitative aspects of China's economic performance.

The future structure of China's economy obviously will comprise a mixture of centrally planned and administered economic activity. There will be a somewhat greater share of decentralized administered economic activity (both planned and unplanned) and a sizable sector of collective and individual economic activities that are carried out according to a mix of planned directives, administrative instructions, and market forces. While these separate categories of economic activities have characterized China's economy since 1949, the center of gravity obviously is swinging away from the mandatory, centrally planned and controlled end of the spectrum and moving toward the decentralized, market forces at the opposite pole. In fact, output decisions even in the planned sector will be influenced by market demand much more often than in the past. These are rather general conclusions, however, and it is far too early to be certain about either the outcome of the present process of economic reform in China or about its impact on China's economic development and trade relations.

Excerpt from the paper by Xu Jiewen

BEGINNING IN 1978, China began to practice the policy of readjustment, reform, consolidation, and improvement of the national economy to invigorate the domestic economy and open itself to the outside world. The reform was first carried out in the countryside. In 1978 Anhui Province began to experiment with a contracted responsibility system, with remuneration linked to work. It distributed to the households the collectively owned land, forest, and other major means of production. Each household managed its production and retained all of its income after paying a state agriculture tax (about 3 percent of the total agricultural income), and a contribution to the public accumulation fund and the public welfare fund (about 6 percent to 7 percent of the total agricultural income). The state purchased the farm and sideline produce according to a certain range of fixed prices, with higher prices paid for above-quota purchases. The rest of the produce was at the disposal of the farmers. This responsibility system linked profits with the farmers' work and management performance. Therefore, this system was well received by the farmers. In 1979 the system began to be introduced throughout the nation, and by 1983, 179.85 million households applied this system, 97.04 percent of the total farming households in China.

While the reform was going on in the rural areas, experimental reforms were also conducted in some cities. First, diversity in economic forms was allowed; in particular, the collective and individual economies were allowed to develop. By 1983 the total number of employees in the collective enterprises of the cities and towns reached 27.44 million, an increase of 34 percent over 1978. The total number of urban individual workers reached 2.31 million, more than fifteen times the number of such workers in 1978. The industrial value created by the collective enterprises was 135.42 billion yuan, a 55.5 percent increase over 1979. The collective enterprises' share in the gross value of industrial output grew from 19 percent in 1979 to 22 percent in 1983.

Second, the system of economic responsibility was applied extensively in state-owned enterprises. Beginning in 1978, some enterprises tried the method of retaining a certain amount of profits. These enterprises were allowed to retain 12 percent to 20 percent of the profits, to be used for expanding production and increasing bonus and welfare subsidies. They were also given some rights over planning, marketing, and cadre appointment and removal. In 1981 quite a number of small- and medium-sized enterprises and a few big ones tried another kind of responsibility system: after an enterprise fulfilled the task of delivering a certain amount of fixed or accumulated profits to the state, it could keep the rest. Beginning in 1983, a new type of practice was introduced: enterprises paid taxes to the state instead of delivering profits. Except for the payment of income tax and other taxes, all or most of the rest of the income would be at the disposal of the enterprise. This practice was accompanied by the expansion of the operating powers of the enterprises. Enterprises had increased authority over planning, marketing, the setting of prices, selection and purchase of products, fund utilization, asset disposal, organizational framework, labor and personnel management, wage and bonus distribution, and joint management. In addition, some small industrial and commercial enterprises owned by the state were run by the collective on a trial basis, leased to or assigned on a contractual basis to individuals, or completely managed by the collective.

In China's macroeconomic policy, there has been a gradual shift from mandatory planning to guidance planning. The past practice of state allocations for investment has been replaced by bank loans, and the prices of some products are allowed to float within certain limits or be completely regulated by the market.

On the whole, these reforms have yielded good results and have promoted the readjustment and development of the national economy. From 1979 to 1983, the average annual increase of total value of social production was 8.2 percent. The average annual growth rates of industrial output, agricultural output, and total value of industrial and agricultural production were all 7.9 percent. National income grew annually by 7.1 percent. By 1983 imbalances in different economic sectors were basically redressed. People's living standards were raised significantly, and the national economy began to embark on a road of stable and healthy progress. In 1983 the share of agriculture, light industry, and heavy industry in the total value of industrial and agricultural output became 33.9 percent, 32.1 percent, and 34.0 percent, respectively. Accumulation decreased to 30.0 percent of the total national income. The average wage for workers and other employees increased 34.5 percent in absolute terms and 15.3 percent in real terms over 1978. However, as the reform is still limited in scope and lacks coordination, the result of the reform is still modest.

Currently, the focus of China's economic reform has been moved from the countryside to the cities. The crux of urban reform lies in the proper handling of the relations among the rights and interests of the state, the collective, and the individual, and in recognizing the relatively independent economic interests of enterprises and workers. Enterprises should be given their proper rights regarding economic management and administration commensurate with their economic interests, so as to bring their initiative into play and enhance the vitality of the whole socialist economy.

The major tasks of the urban reform are to establish a strict system of economic responsibility, break away from the practice of "everybody eating from the same rice bowl" (that is, extreme egalitarianism), implement the principle of distribution according to work, and ensure that the interests and rights of workers are linked with their responsibilities. Such a system calls for the reform of the distribution system, labor policies, the price system, the planning structure, and the functions of the state.

In the field of distribution, relations between the state and the enterprise have been basically redefined with the replacement of the mandatory delivery of profits by a system of taxes paid to the state. Now comes a task of paramount importance: wage reform to ensure that the overall amount of wages in an enterprise rises in accordance with its improved economic performance (although the index for enterprise efficiency is still to be determined), and that employees' wages rise with their personal contributions and the economic progress of their enterprise. A statewide wage system for administrative offices still exists, including fringe

benefits and bonuses. This system will be reformed to increase
the differences between skilled and unskilled labor. Wage reform
calls for a widened difference between mental and manual, complex
and simple, skilled and unskilled, and heavy and light work.
Wages are to play the role of rewarding the diligent and punishing
the lazy by giving more pay for more work and less pay for less
work.

Along with wage reform, it is necessary to reform the labor
system by introducing a system of labor contracts and developing
new measures for cadre recruitment. Under the guidance of state
policies and plans, workers can choose their own jobs so as to
secure a free flow of personnel, and enterprises can enroll workers
through exams.

At present, uniform state prices are still predominant, but in
the future these will be replaced mainly or even completely by
prices that float within certain limits or are set wholly by market
forces. Price reform will ensure that prices respond promptly to
the changes in value and in the relationship between supply and
demand so as to meet the needs of national economic development.

In planning, it is necessary to reduce the scope of mandatory
planning and extend the scope of guidance planning. Guidance
planning means the use of economic levers, such as the adjustment
of prices, tax rates, and interest rates, and market mechanisms to
encourage enterprises to achieve state goals on a voluntary basis.
Mandatory planning will be applied to major products that have
a direct bearing on the national economy and people's livelihood,
and these products will not be subject to guidance planning until
conditions are ripe. At present, 20 percent to 30 percent of
industrial output is subject to mandatory planning, but we will
try to limit mandatory planning further in the future. However,
even when applying mandatory planning, we should exchange
goods on the basis of their value.

In administration and management, it is necessary to expand
the role of enterprises and workers and to enlarge management
and decisionmaking power at various levels. The functions of the
state in managing the economy are limited to the following:
formulating the guidelines, policies, regulations and plans, and
supervising their execution; coordinating economic relations among
localities and departments; collecting a part of enterprise income
through various taxes; appointing or enrolling chief leaders of
enterprises; making decisions on the establishment, closing, or
merging of enterprises; shifting to another line of production; or
stopping production altogether. The concrete issues of manage-

ment and administration are left to the enterprises. Bound by the precondition of having to implement state policies, laws, and plans, enterprises are entitled to choose the forms of management, labor, and wages and bonuses. They can also arrange freely the supply, production, and marketing of goods, using the funds they retain. They can fix product prices and appoint, remove, recruit, or elect their staff. Inside an enterprise, the system of having directors (or managers) assume responsibility is practiced, and the party organizations play only the role of supervisor and guarantor. While practicing this system, it is essential to set up the system of workers' congresses and formulate regulations for democratic management. With the reform, enterprises should become relatively independent economic entities in which staff and workers are masters.

An economy based on the public ownership of the means of production is the main force in China's socialist economy, but China cannot develop only this kind of economy. In light of actual conditions, China must vigorously promote the collective economy, the individual economy, joint ventures, and wholly foreign owned enterprises along with the state economy. Moreover, China should actively promote flexible cooperative management and economic unions between state, collective, and individually owned enterprises. Some small, publicly owned enterprises should be leased to or run by collectives or individuals on a contractual basis. Competition should be allowed among economic forms, managerial approaches, departments, and enterprises, subjecting them to the judgment and test of consumers in the market, and ensuring that only the best will survive.

These reforms have drawn some useful experience from the capitalist economies, for example, the use of market mechanisms and economic levers. But the reforms will not lead to capitalism or a "mixed economy." Market mechanisms and economic levers are integral parts of any commodity economy. The capitalist economy is one form of the commodity economy, but it is not the only form. The socialist planned economy is a planned commodity economy.

Comments

AMERICAN PARTICIPANT. I see two problems with reform. I am pessimistic about tax reform as long as there is an adjustment tax, whereby the amount of taxes an enterprise pays is not based completely on its efficiency. The other problem concerns wage reform. It appears that no one will get a wage cut, but there will be increases for those workers who possess specific skills that are in demand. The only way of avoiding inequality in such a situation is to allow free mobility of labor, creating a permanent shift from rural to urban areas. Many Chinese scholars agree with the need for this mobility, but no official Chinese statement mentions the free flow of labor among regions, only within an enterprise or within a firm.

CHINESE PARTICIPANT. China's conditions and comparative advantages, especially its human resources, must be considered when discussing China's growth. There must be labor mobility, and in the last few years we have encouraged this, especially for skilled labor. We have set up bureaus as clearinghouses for labor. When the wishes of the individual and his work unit coincide, then he can move. There may also be a scenario in which the worker may still be allowed to move even though the work unit is reluctant to change the status quo. Whenever there is mobility, the danger of friction between the interests of the firm and the individual arises. The problem with firing workers is that the present social security system is linked to a person's job. Without another social security safety net, there should be no right to fire workers except for those who commit crimes. A comprehensive safety net has to be established along with labor mobility.

At the end of the Cultural Revolution, China had 100 percent mandatory planning. A gradual reduction in the scope of mandatory planning continues. For example, in Wuhan and Guangzhou, vegetables are sold at market prices, and only 50 percent to 80 percent of steel output is governed by mandatory planning.

CHINESE PARTICIPANT. I do not think mandatory planning will be eliminated, at least in my lifetime, although its scope will be decreased.

CHINESE PARTICIPANT. In academic circles, one school believes mandatory planning can be removed, the other does not. Ultimately, it will depend on future developments, since academic debate does not reflect official policy. Enterprise production falls into the categories of state, negotiated, and market prices, with state-set prices being predominant. Oil is sold under a fixed price, steel is not. Only eighty products are presently under mandatory plans. We will continue to use guidance planning and economic measures even if our goals are not met. If necessary, the state will raise the selling price, offer preferential tax treatment, or give lower interest rates to achieve production targets. We will not force enterprises to produce unprofitable products but will use measures to make it profitable for those goods to be produced.

AMERICAN PARTICIPANT. At what point would the current reforms become irreversible? I believe under four conditions: first, when the people resist any reversal, believing that the present policy benefits them; second, when all groups within the party completely agree on the desirability of present policy; third, when the reforms have been in place for an indefinite period without impediment; and fourth, when the reforms take root institutionally and those institutions acquire a vested interest in the continuation of the reforms. Unfortunately, all four conditions are probably immeasurable except in hindsight.

CHINESE PARTICIPANT. I share your concern over the lack of discussion of politics in our consideration of China's economic reforms thus far. The peasants are already solidly behind the reforms. The current party rectification will unify the party on the direction of reforms. It will take perhaps twenty to thirty years before institutional change is complete, owing to our trial-and-error methods. The entire reform package will not be reversed because nearly all benefit from higher wages. All the reforms are experimental, and some of them may be modified, but the package will not be abandoned. The issue is how far economic reform will be allowed to affect the entire social system, so perhaps the more relevant question to ask is what aspects of the reforms are most likely to face objections and by whom.

CHINESE PARTICIPANT. Some Chinese are unhappy about the reforms because decentralization takes away their power, but most Chinese benefit from them. I believe that the reforms are irreversible because reform has the support of the majority of the Chinese people and because the problems that will arise will be easy to resolve.

CHINESE PARTICIPANT. All Chinese support the reforms and will go along with them even after Deng, Hu, and Zhao are gone. The reforms have not encountered resistance, only inertia. The reforms will exist forever.

CHINESE PARTICIPANT. We have committed leftist errors in the past few decades that the cadres, workers, and farmers will not tolerate any more. Everybody hates egalitarianism. We are now redressing our past mistakes and above all the mistake of class struggle. Our reforms have been more successful and spectacular than in the Soviet Union and Eastern Europe because we have the full support of the people: the peasants initiated the reforms in the rural areas and the city dwellers initiated the reforms now beginning in the urban areas. Experimental reforms in the cities or provinces encourage other areas to demand the same reforms.

CHINESE PARTICIPANT. There is no guarantee except success. The success of the reforms has both internal and external factors, so we must be cautious and avoid committing mistakes to ensure the success of the reforms. There indeed is resistance, but it is not significant.

The "Open Economy" Policy

Excerpt from the paper by Xu Jiewen

SINCE 1979, a series of reforms has been introduced to the structure of China's external economic management. First, special economic zones in Shenzhen, Xiaman, Zhuhai, and Shantou were established, fourteen coastal cities and Hainan Island were opened, and coastal economic development zones were set up in the Yangtze Delta, Pearl River Delta, and Mingnan Delta. These cities and regions can be considered China's "land of gold." The population of the fourteen coastal cities is only about 5 percent of the country's total, yet their value of industrial output is about one-fourth of the nation's total, and Shanghai's value of industrial output alone accounts for approximately one-sixth of the nation's total.

Second, we reformed the foreign trade structure. Since 1979, China has delegated more management power to various trade departments and tried the agent system for import and export. By 1984 there were 548 foreign trade enterprises in the central departments and provinces, of which 430 were set up after 1979. There are 254 trade offices abroad, of which 248 were set up after 1979. The state-controlled trade system has been replaced by a multichanneled system with unified leadership and relative independence and various forms of business transactions.

The foreign trade system will undergo an all-around reform along the same lines as the urban reforms. Government administration should be separated from enterprise management. State trade departments will only be responsible for the administration and control of the macrostructure of foreign trade. Trade enterprises will be responsible for the concrete business management and become economic entities with independent business accounting and sole responsibility for profits and losses, rather than appendages of the administrative departments. An agent system will be applied extensively to both imports and exports. A system of strict economic responsibility will be set up in all foreign trade enterprises, and professional management will be practiced by integrating industry or technology with trade and combining imports with exports. Guidance planning will also be applied to foreign trade, in which the state employs the levers of tax, price, credit, and so forth to regulate imports and exports. We will enhance our economic effectiveness in foreign trade and strengthen

China's economic relations with other countries through these reforms.

Third, more flexible policies have been adopted and a series of external economic regulations and laws have been promulgated. These reforms have promoted the growth of China's external economic relations. China's total trade volume more than doubled between 1978 and 1983, with an average annual growth rate of 16.2 percent. Yet these are still initial reforms, and state monopoly of foreign trade has not been replaced. The practice of state trade enterprises taking care of profits and losses remains unchanged. As a result, economic effectiveness is still very low in foreign trade.

Excerpt from the paper by Robert F. Dernberger

THE CHANGE IN China's developmental strategy is referred to as the creation of an "open economy." While it does encourage a considerably higher rate of participation in foreign trade than in the past, the borrowing of foreign loans on a considerably larger scale than in the past, and the unprecedented attempt to stimulate direct foreign investment in the People's Republic of China, the new open economy policy still falls far short of the open economy policies of the NICs. The reform of the foreign sector, however, is still unfolding, and the opening of the economy to direct foreign investment and its rapid growth in the foreseeable future is a logical outcome of many recent developments. The first step in the reform of the foreign trade sector was the mere increase in the level of foreign trade, that is, the significant increase in the ratio of China's foreign trade to its GNP. The decentralization of decisionmaking on foreign trade followed, and, eventually, the elimination of the state's foreign trade monopolies took place. In other words, local levels of government, the economic administration, and even enterprises can directly participate in foreign trade transactions. Next came the borrowing of foreign loans and, eventually, allowing lower levels of the government, the economic administration, and even enterprises to engage in foreign borrowing—again, under strict control and centrally established guidelines.

A third and novel step was the creation of four special economic zones and the granting of special rights to two provinces for participation in foreign trade and investment activities. The special economic zones were created in undeveloped areas on the coast and were to be similar to foreign trade zones in other countries. Tariff and tax exemptions were granted to foreign-owned enterprises created in these zones, but the output of these enterprises was to be sold abroad, not in the domestic economy. For the possible role of direct foreign investment in the Chinese economy in the future, however, the most recent development is perhaps the most significant: allowing several Chinese cities (initially, the list included fourteen cities) to grant foreigners special concessions (not as great as those granted by the special economic zones) and to exercise greater control over their own participation in foreign trade and foreign borrowing and investment. The arrangements made by the central government vary, but each city can now make its own arrangements with foreigners for loans and projects up to certain monetary limits. As a result, each of these cities is creating "technology" parks, industrial parks, and residential areas for foreigners and is actively competing for foreign loans, technology agreements, and foreign investment. The key problem remains whether or not the foreign enterprise can sell its output on the domestic market, but partnership in a Chinese enterprise is a possible way around this problem.

The open economy policy should remain as a basic change in development strategy and therefore China's foreign trade dependency will continue to increase; exports and imports will increase faster than national income. But China is not a NIC, nor is it likely to become one, considering the proportion of its population engaged in agriculture, the percentage of its foreign trade dependency, its human resources, and other factors, although the income per capita may be the same. Capital inflows will also continue to grow as a share of domestic investment, but the share of foreign loans in the total will decline, while the growth will be the result of increased direct foreign investment. These direct foreign investments will be forthcoming only if the foreigner is allowed to participate in the domestic economy, that is, to invest in production facilities within the Chinese economy that produce goods and services for sale in the Chinese market; and if the Chinese create a legal system and use it to assure the foreigner of recourse to legal judgments in the face of the foreigner's need to work with a bureaucracy with a tradition of decisionmaking based on personal relations, not codified rules and laws. It is still too early to declare with any certainty that these two conditions will be met.

Excerpt from the paper by Rachel McCulloch

IN THE CHINESE economy, the main element currently luring foreign investors into joint ventures is the large and growing domestic market. However, Chinese officials are understandably concerned about generating foreign exchange, so that negotiations tend to stress production for export rather than for the domestic market. Moreover, the domestic economic and political environment poses substantial risks. Local inputs are of uncertain quality, and many investors have experienced delivery delays. The legal and administrative framework within which joint ventures must operate is still taking shape, and the potential remains for at least a partial reversal in the current open economic policy.

Despite a continuing ambivalence about foreign participation in efforts to modernize the Chinese economy, the government has produced a flurry of new regulations intended to improve the environment for equity joint ventures and other forms of foreign involvement. These measures include laws directly affecting operations of foreign firms, as well as broader efforts to improve the functioning of the Chinese economy through substitution of incentive systems for rigid administrative controls. The result is an unprecedented level of foreign activity in virtually every industrial sector, with almost daily announcements of proposed joint ventures between local enterprises and multinational firms based in the United States, Japan, Europe, and even other developing nations.

An obvious prerequisite for continued progress along current lines is a working domestic political consensus favoring the outward-looking approach to modernization, rather than a return to the xenophobia and near autarky fostered under Mao. As the new leadership grapples with the apparent conflicts between recent reforms and Marxist ideology and between the open economic policy and the ultimate goal of national self-reliance, the appropriate role of profit-oriented enterprises, whether Chinese or foreign, in socialist development remains contentious.

Comments

AMERICAN PARTICIPANT. Doubt over the ability of foreign partners to repatriate profits is one of the primary limitations on the willingness of foreign firms to invest in China. But some companies have found solutions to this problem. The 3M company has a wholly owned subsidiary in China that produces solely for the domestic market. To repatriate profits, 3M has created a separate joint venture purchasing company with S. Shamash and Sons, Inc., a New York-based firm with long experience in the China trade, especially as an importer of silk. This purchasing company uses profits earned from sales to China's domestic market to buy goods produced in Shanghai, which are then exported and sold abroad. Chinese regulations require that goods exported through this sort of arrangement must be goods not already exported by China.[2]

AMERICAN PARTICIPANT. A distinction must be drawn between profits earned in foreign exchange, the repatriation of which is guaranteed by the joint venture law (although there is some question about its timely implementation) and profits earned in *renminbi,* the Chinese currency. The question for the latter case is whether foreign companies that earn renminbi by selling to China's domestic market can convert their profits into U.S. dollars and repatriate them. The answer I heard during a recent visit to China was that the foreign firm would be encouraged to exchange its profits for Chinese goods and thus would earn back its foreign exchange by the sale of those goods overseas. I did not hear the further complication that was just mentioned—that these goods must be ones that would otherwise not be exported. One of the problems of the Shenzhen special economic zone is that the Hong Kong dollar has driven the renminbi out of circulation. One reason for this occurrence is the concern of the Hong Kong investors, many of whom operate in the hotel and restaurant sector, about their right to repatriate their renminbi profits. But if those profits are earned in Hong Kong dollars, they can literally be carried out of Shenzhen, avoiding any question about the convertibility of profits.

AMERICAN PARTICIPANT. Taking commodities as compensation is not uncommon. This is normally done with Eastern Europe. But it is still complex.

CHINESE PARTICIPANT. Joint venture profits derived from exporting can all be repatriated by using the foreign exchange earned from export sales. However, it is not necessary to rely only on exports to earn foreign exchange for the repatriation of profit. Joint ventures can also sell on the domestic market if their goods are needed or if the venture provides technology that is much needed in China. Joint venture goods procured by China's domestic firms may be paid for with foreign exchange.

AMERICAN PARTICIPANT. The United States has a fairly liberal trade policy because it feels it is good for the country and the welfare of its citizens. China, in the past, only traded to have a minimal level of imports as determined by central planners. China often appears to believe that exports are ends in themselves even if they are not used to buy imports. Who should determine the level of imports: central planners, individual enterprises, or con-

2. See Andrew S. Heyden, "The Silk Road to Countertrade," *China Business Review,* vol. 12 (March-April 1985), pp. 6–7.

sumers? Liberalization, in the United States, is for the benefit of consumers. Is this also true for China?

CHINESE PARTICIPANT. Trade decentralization leaves decisions about imports to the enterprises, who must base their decisions solely on price signals to make a profit for themselves and the state. Therefore, the decentralization of trade decisions in China requires the existence of rational domestic prices. We must ensure that the state price is correct and that there is a balance between supply and demand. Falsely low prices lead to greater imports and profits on paper only. China is now trying to readjust prices, but this process may take four to five years. Until the readjustment is complete, it is impossible to liberalize trade as fully as others would like because, under present circumstances, trade liberalization will not benefit China.

No country wishes to put itself in a vulnerable position through its trade policies. Its economic activities must not be dependent on world involvement. China cannot be dependent on foreign trade with its current set of irrational prices, and even after the price reform is completed it will not become dependent because China will demand the right of state intervention in its trading practices to protect itself from monopolistic tendencies in the world.

CHINESE PARTICIPANT. China has a potentially large market, but it is now at a low level. It is unrealistic to expect China to open its market and increase imports because it is no more able to absorb manufactured goods from the developed countries than are other developing countries. Even after price readjustments, China will require overall restrictions on trade. China will not allow free trade because it needs the right of state intervention; even Japan exercises this right. China's ability to absorb direct foreign investment will depend on the overall economy: infrastructure, telecommunications, water supply, transportation, industrial plant, and so forth. There is no point in hastening foreign investment without that infrastructure.

AMERICAN PARTICIPANT. The real problem of protectionism is at the margin: in which direction is a country moving? I do not think anyone would say that the United States is a protectionist country today; the question is, in what direction is it moving? China has not applied an "open economy" philosophy to the determination of its imports. China does not protect only infant industries, but also protects stagnant industries that are more than thirty years old. In many areas, goods that are already made in China cannot be imported, even if it is more efficient to do so.

AMERICAN PARTICIPANT. How will China define infant industries? It is hard to call large industries that are thirty years old infant industries. China needs to choose imports on the basis of what industries it wishes to protect. One result of not importing certain goods is the protection of inefficient industries. What is the academic view in China on this issue?

CHINESE PARTICIPANT. It is hard to define an infant industry. All industries in China are infants compared with those in developed countries. The steel industry is in the process of change and cannot be made competitive with developed countries. Not all industries in developing countries should be protected. In China, we had no world competition and so our industries are inefficient. This situation should not continue, which is why we are opening our market in a systematic way.

CHINESE PARTICIPANT. All countries protect their own industries during the beginning of industrialization. This is connected to some extent to the development of labor-intensive infant industries, but the two processes are not identical. Labor-intensive industry in developing countries includes some infant industries, such as television and electronics, whereas in developed countries labor intensive refers mostly to assembly. No one single product can be seen as of one type or the other. Steel may be capital intensive, but it can also use computers and advanced technology. In the 1950s Japan protected certain industries, although not all, and then loosened controls as they developed. China has adopted some protectionism to allow internal competition, but it does not limit the import of the most advanced technology.

CHINESE PARTICIPANT. The characteristics of an infant industry are the following: first, it uses little energy, whereas traditional industries use much energy; second, it is technology intensive; third, it has broad connections with the market, and marketing is more complicated than with traditional goods; and fourth, it produces higher value-added goods.

AMERICAN PARTICIPANT. There is a distinction between new and infant industries. A new industry is one that produces a newly developed product for the world market, such as computers, while infant industries represent a new industry for the home country and are usually in developing countries, although not always. The question is, for how long is protection of new and infant industries justified? Since China is a command economy with irrational prices, it is hard to know whether one is protecting an infant industry or merely an inefficient one.

CHINESE PARTICIPANT. China has two forms of protectionism:

for infant industries and for old and backward industries. It is difficult to define an infant industry, even in a command economy. Our petrochemical industry is not as efficient as in other countries. We calculate the costs, and it is possibly better to export oil and import petrochemicals, but then our own industry would never develop. We must have a timetable for protectionism and for catching up with the developed countries.

AMERICAN PARTICIPANT. A definition of infant industries must include the ability to learn by doing, wherein experience will result in lower costs. But more preconditions must be met for the policy of protectionism, because a country will incur great costs during the period of protectionism. If the benefits of eventual competitiveness cannot outweigh the costs, protectionism is not economically justified in terms of the country's own narrow interests, leaving aside the effects on the rest of the world. And at present rates of interest, protectionism is not likely to be economically rational. For instance, if the American shoe industry can become competitive within five years, why does venture capital not rush to the industry? Because even in those five years, the gains from becoming competitive will not be worth the cost.

AMERICAN PARTICIPANT. China's economy is projected to grow at 7 percent to 8 percent for some time and has grown by 8 percent during the last eight years. This rate will let China's economy double and quadruple very rapidly. China has sustained high growth rates for several decades. It has been growing at a rate and from a base similar to South Korea and Hong Kong. It will certainly become a NIC by any definition, but a much larger one than we are used to. What is the significance of this development to the rest of the world? What is the impact on foreign trade? Large countries do not trade as much as small countries, such as South Korea and Taiwan, do. China's foreign trade has been growing at about 20 percent each year. Does this growth imply an enormous trade power in the future? The total trade of China, Taiwan, and Hong Kong is about $160 billion, half of Japan's trade, and all of them have very high growth. If the three of them are combined as a single economic unit in the future, they will certainly be a major economic power. In the long run, China's debt is a small percentage of its exports. It could borrow about $8 billion a year for several years without any problems.

AMERICAN PARTICIPANT. The foreign exchange constraint on China's economy and its balance of payments problems can be eased with borrowing and direct foreign investment, just as a province's internal trade deficit with other provinces is offset by transferring capital from other regions of the country. Guangdong may not need a balance of trade in its trade with other regions in China because it can draw savings from the rest of the country to balance its current account. This imbalance does not cause concern because we believe there are benefits to both Guangdong and to the rest of China while that imbalance of domestic trade is occurring. Applying this idea to China's relationship with the rest of the world is more difficult because China's renminbi is different from other foreign currencies, but the analogy with the domestic economy does hold. It would make sense, for some lengthy transitional period, for China to run a sizable current account deficit, financed by attracting savings from the rest of the world. This could occur through either direct borrowing or direct foreign investment, both of which have their advantages.

China needs to consider borrowing as an alternative to direct foreign investment and licensing. If we look at other countries and their development, there are some instructive examples of countries that ran a large current account deficit for many years and did not have balanced trade. This was true of the United States, Australia, and New Zealand in the nineteenth century. The current account deficit as a proportion of gross domestic product (GDP) was very large. Singapore has had a current account deficit of 7 percent to 9 percent of GDP, which has been financed by capital flows of direct foreign investment and borrowing that eased the constraints of foreign exchange reserves. There are obvious differences between countries like Singapore and China, and we know from the experience of Brazil and Mexico that difficulties are associated with foreign borrowing, especially if the rest of the world experiences economic turbulence. But I wonder if it is really important for China to always have a favorable balance of trade. This concern is related to the question of the link between the repatriation of profits and exports. If they are always linked together, then you are tying imports to exports and you lose some important flexibility in raising foreign exchange.

Excerpt from the paper by Rachel McCulloch

OF THE MANY important decisions taken by Chinese officials since announcement of the four modernizations (industry, agriculture, science and technology, and national defense) program, the choice of promoting direct foreign investment to gain access to advanced technology is arguably the most striking departure from past practice. More than any of the domestic reforms to decentralize key economic decisions and replace administrative controls by incentives, this choice represents a move beyond even the most ambitious experiments of Eastern bloc countries.

China's leadership has clearly recognized that access to advanced technology is central to the economic performance and growth prospects of any nation, regardless of its economic philosophy. In almost every country, access has been achieved through a mixture of indigenous research and development (R&D) and technology transfer, that is, the importation of the fruits of successful foreign R&D efforts.

Comments

AMERICAN PARTICIPANT. China's definition of direct foreign investment is different from that of other countries: it includes ventures with foreign involvement but without foreign equity. I agree that what distinguishes such investment is that there is some foreign control, whether or not it is linked to equity ownership. Technology transfer and direct foreign investment range from a one-time, one-item sale to a wholly owned, operated, and managed foreign enterprise with intimate links with the host country. In comparison with domestic firms, foreign firms in a foreign country have an inherent disadvantage: legal discrimination, cultural ignorance, and lack of links to domestic supply networks. The advantage is their more advanced technology, including marketing know-how as well as the manufacturing process.

The advantages of investing in China are not all they are said to be: it is true that China has many natural resources, a large internal market, and potentially cheap labor. But direct foreign investment is possible only if foreigners agree to emphasize exports, and China's low wages are offset by the low productivity of its labor; moreover, a premium wage is paid by the foreign firm that is not received by the workers.

Excerpt from the paper by Rachel McCulloch

TO EVALUATE the role of direct foreign investment as a mode of technology transfer, it is useful to consider the full range of methods through which China potentially can gain access to advanced technology. Not surprisingly, certain modes of transfer are complementary, and reliance on a combination of these methods is superior to the selection of only one. In other cases, modes are fundamentally substitutes, institutional forms with different advantages and disadvantages.

The most basic and essential way a nation gains access to advanced scientific and technical knowledge from abroad is through education and training. Chinese policymakers have fully appreciated this fact. Given the recent disruption of the domestic educational system during the Cultural Revolution, the goal of upgrading education and training has required sending large numbers of students and scholars abroad. Presumably, a larger part of educational needs can be met through domestic schooling once the nation's colleges, universities, and technical schools have been restored to full operation. However, this process will take years, since it entails the training abroad of adequate faculty.

Most training abroad is of a general character, not specific to particular industrial processes or products. Specific technical knowledge, perhaps better labeled know-how, is usually gained through learning by doing or on-the-job training. In other developing nations, this process has normally meant training that is connected with production in local subsidiaries of foreign firms, although contracts with foreign firms for training of local workers have increased in importance. Local regulation of direct foreign investment may stipulate minimum acceptable levels of training activities, either directly or through requirements for local participation in various managerial functions.

It is widely recognized that general education is not only in itself a mode of technology transfer but also the most important determinant of the "absorptive capacity" of a technology-importing nation. But it is a complement to, not a substitute for, the kind of know-how that may be obtained through appropriate direct foreign investment.

A more difficult question concerns the substitution of training contracts (or management contracts) for direct investments—in other words, unbundling foreign economic relations to obtain training without foreign equity interest. The problem of monitoring the "product" arises in an arrangement of this type. In a foreign investment, trainees must satisfy the operational needs of the foreign firm, which provides a type of internal quality control, although neither the nature of the training nor the number of workers trained may be entirely satisfactory from the Chinese perspective. No such mechanism for quality control is an inherent part of a training contract.

One important determinant of the extent of training undertaken by foreign investors is the likelihood that workers, once trained, will move on to other employment. If the likelihood is high, the value of such training to the firm is obviously reduced, although its social value is unaffected or even increased. Legal arrangements fostering apprenticeship or similar contractual arrangements between employer and trainee can reduce the conflict. A different approach is regulation that fosters employment of local workers in all or most aspects of the operation. In such an environment, training is encouraged but not necessarily required; if mobility is high, at least some of the training is likely to be undertaken by independent tuition-financed operations.

Recruitment from abroad of skilled workers and entrepreneurs is another strategy used with varying success in promoting development in Latin America and, more recently, in oil-exporting nations. In China, similar efforts have centered on ethnic Chinese in the industrialized nations and other developing areas. It is reasonable to assume that this group has cultural affinity and, in many cases, direct family ties with China.

Since the potential quantitative impact of this strategy is relatively small, it may be more important as a symbol of China's reintegration into the world community than as a lever for technological advancement. On the other hand, ethnic Chinese entrepreneurs and managers may be at an advantage over other foreigners seeking to enter the newly open door of Chinese industry. Numerically, for instance, Hong Kong firms account for the lion's share of joint ventures established in China since 1978.

Licensing agreements are often one element in a direct investment package, but they can also constitute an arm's-length, contractual arrangement for the use of technology. Japan's impressive technological advancement proceeded mainly along this route, and such agreements are commonplace among firms in the advanced industrial nations. The presumed advantages of licensing are greater local control and the ability to obtain desired technologies at lower cost.

For a nation at China's current stage of technological development, the licensing option seems less promising. Indigenous legal and technological expertise is essential in establishing mutually beneficial contractual terms and in integrating the new technology into the national economy. This required expertise is precisely what China is not yet in a position to supply.

Compensation trade and processing agreements, similar to supply agreements negotiated by American and Western European firms in Eastern Europe, have been used in various light manufacturing activities. These modes are particularly attractive in socialist economies because there is no foreign ownership and typically no required foreign exchange payments for machinery or inputs. Moreover, long-term export contracts could have some of the same learning-by-doing benefits for Chinese enterprises as does direct foreign investment.

The technologies involved are ones not usually ranked as advanced. Nonetheless, such agreements can facilitate integration of modern tools and machinery into local enterprises. Often more important, they serve as conduits through which Chinese workers and managers gain know-how about organization of production, incentive systems, quality control, and marketing. Managerial skills are areas of notable weakness in China and other socialist economies, in part because of their past policy of deemphasizing production of consumer goods.

With far greater flexibility and much less foreign control over local operations, this type of arrangement is basically a complement to direct foreign investment rather than an alternative. Like indigenous R&D, processing agreements tend to expand the Chinese economy's capacity to absorb advanced technologies from abroad.

In contrast to the wholly owned subsidiary, a joint venture is a type of direct investment in which enterprises of at least two nations have an equity interest or substantive managerial role. In a sense, every foreign investment is a joint venture, since the host government has a legal claim to both a share of the profits and a voice in management (and often the formal foreign partner is a government-owned entity). Thus it is probably better to view the difference between a wholly owned subsidiary and a joint venture as a matter of degree, with a joint venture implying a more substantial sharing of profits or of managerial control over operations.

In contemporary China, the joint venture is likely to be the dominant form of direct foreign investment. Such investments are permitted under the "Law on Joint Ventures Using Chinese and Foreign Investment," adopted in 1979. This law specifies that the foreign partner must supply a minimum of 25 percent of the equity but stipulates no maximum, so wholly owned subsidiaries are implicitly allowed. However, wholly owned subsidiaries have so far been concentrated in the special economic zones, where foreign investments are subject to different regulations.

Although joint ventures are a recent and dramatic innovation for China, considerable evidence has accumulated about their role in other host countries. The fact that firms with technological advantages will prefer to exploit them through direct investment rather than arm's-length modes implies a preference for a wholly owned subsidiary over a joint venture. And, as noted, dilution of the foreign investor's equity and control changes managerial incentives, especially if a joint venture is not the parent's preferred involvement in the host country. In particular, making joint ventures the norm may reduce the contribution of proprietary technology by multinational investors and could even deter some firms from entering the market.

On the other hand, the parent may have economic or cultural

reasons, quite apart from the policies of the host nation, for seeking joint venture arrangements. Japanese multinationals are much more prone to participate in joint ventures than are their U.S. or European counterparts. This, and their extensive experience in other Asian NICs, may give them an advantage over their Western competitors in entering China's open door.

China has also begun to establish joint ventures abroad. Like joint ventures in China, these operations may allow Chinese managers to improve their skills in various aspects of production and marketing and to gain information about superior technologies. However, such partnerships are possible only if the potential Chinese partner can bring into the venture something of value. For successful foreign firms, China's financial contribution itself would not provide sufficient inducement. The most likely foreign partners in such ventures are those in financial difficulty and those seeking access to the Chinese market through this channel.

Excerpt from the paper by Wang Zengzhuang

THE CHINESE government and people regard the acquisition of modern science and technology suited to China's conditions as the key to the banishment of poverty and backwardness and the realization of the four modernizations; consequently, the policy has been formulated to rely on scientific and technological progress in developing the economy vigorously, while the development of science and technology must be oriented toward economic construction.

In raising the level of its science and technology rapidly and accelerating economic growth, a big country like China naturally has to depend mainly on its own efforts. Yet the experience of China and other countries has impressed upon us that we must be open to the outside world, participate in the worldwide endeavor for economic growth and scientific-technological progress, and learn and import the advanced technologies of other countries, while at the same time continuing to rely primarily on our own efforts. Thus, since early 1979, China has pursued a policy of opening to the outside world and made great efforts to carry out international economic and technical cooperation in various forms, striving to speed up its socialist construction as much as possible by using foreign funds, introducing advanced technology, and expanding foreign trade.

Over the last few years, along with the introduction and implementation of the open economic policy, the Chinese government has adopted many important measures and steps aimed at promoting China's economic and trade ties with other countries, including the importation of foreign capital and technology. Since 1979, China has drawn up and promulgated a series of laws, regulations, and bylaws; restored or established ties of credit cooperation with foreign governments and international financial institutions; signed agreements with some foreign countries for the protection of investment and the avoidance of double taxation; and accepted foreign loans and direct investment by foreign capital. China has established four special economic zones, opened up fourteen coastal or port cities as well as Hainan Island, and recently set up three coastal economic development zones, with a view to opening up the entire coastal belt with a population of 200 million.

China offers vast prospects for foreign capital and technology, principally because it has an ideal environment for investment with its rich natural resources, huge potential domestic market, low wage scale, and stable political situation. What is more, in the second half of the 1980s, with low economic growth forecast for the capitalist world, the developed countries will have to seek further outlets for their surplus capital and products, whereas the steady development of the Chinese economy after implementing economic structural reforms will enable China to attract and absorb even more foreign capital and technology. In this regard, China has formulated and introduced realistic policies and measures, drawing on its own practice during the last few years and learning from both the positive and negative experience of the Asian-Pacific region.

China is both a big socialist power and an economically backward developing country; it has rich natural and human resources on the one hand and numerous projects waiting to be built or updated on the other. These circumstances must be taken into account when examining sources of foreign capital and technology. It follows that a multichannel, multidimensional policy should be pursued in utilizing foreign funds and introducing foreign technologies, and extending ties with countries throughout the world, especially those of the Asian-Pacific region, absorbing whatever is best suited to China's needs.

Importation of foreign capital should go hand in hand with the transfer of foreign technology, for technology is even more scarce than foreign capital and is necessary for developing countries, including China. As far as direct foreign investment is concerned, China prefers projects entailing advanced technology and methods of management. Foreign investors who have introduced advanced technology will be permitted to sell part or even all of their products in China's domestic market.

Importing capital and technology on a selective basis is essential. Discretion must be used in selecting what types of foreign capital to use for what purposes. For a developing country like China, securing more long-term and medium-term loans at low or moderate interest and maintaining a rational structure of foreign funding are imperative. In selecting advanced foreign technologies, a country must proceed from economic and technical actualities. China must either concentrate on importing technologies that are suited to its needs and will play a decisive role in updating China's technology and accelerating modernization or stress the technologies that take less investment, give quicker returns, and are conducive to improving China's import-export patterns and increasing foreign exchange earnings. Importance should also be attached, in importing technology, to reducing the consumption of energy and other natural resources and to ensuring a maximum reduction or even elimination of environmental pollution and ecological damage.

China will select whatever methods of importing foreign capital and technology that are suitable to its needs from among various international practices, based on the merits of each case. China will encourage and welcome such practices as joint stock ventures, cooperative operations, cooperative development or production, compensation trade, trade by license, and advisory, consultancy, and technical services. The importation of whole plants, which prevailed in the past as the chief method for introducing foreign technology, will no longer be practiced on a large scale. The integration of trade with technology transfer and the purchase of advanced equipment, which includes the simultaneous transfer of technical know-how, seem better suited to China's needs and will be adopted on a large scale.

Comments   AMERICAN PARTICIPANT. Foreign investment will have some role in China's development and some investors will make profits, but neither investments nor profits will be large. China is simply too different from other markets. Even with the current reforms, there will be problems and limited opportunities. There will have to be specific areas of interest to foreign businesses, such as offshore oil, but at the same time I do not believe the Chinese leaders want large amounts of foreign investment. Furthermore, if the rates of profit become large enough to attract large amounts of investment, it will be easy for the Chinese to restrict those profits.

Should China stress direct foreign investment, even with all the problems that could arise? Perhaps the Chinese should instead emphasize licensing and management contracts, as did South Korea and Japan after World War II.

Chinese students in the United States are more important to China's development than technology transfer because China is not inclined to import human resources as technical aid. China still has an "equipment fetish" and imports all kinds of equipment, whether or not it has people capable of using them efficiently. In this respect, it is very much like the other East Asian countries, with the exception of Singapore and Hong Kong.

CHINESE PARTICIPANT. China wishes to import technology and open its economy, but this process cannot be dissociated from the issue of "brains." Without human resources, technology transfer is only buying equipment. Even in this area, developed countries adopt unfair policies. Their immigration policies attract the technically skilled and restrict the immigration of untalented people.

AMERICAN PARTICIPANT. I agree with my Chinese colleague about the importance of developing human resources, so I am rather surprised by his comments about the United States. The American offer to educate large numbers of Chinese with modern technology may be the greatest single contribution made by the United States to China's modernization.

AMERICAN PARTICIPANT. The Wuhan steel rolling mill, supplied by West Germany, is sophisticated but is run improperly. While I visited the plant, I saw that batches of steel were not sent down fast enough or steadily. The mill also had an inventory of three months or more. The important problem for China is knowing how to maximize existing technology and learning how to use transferred technology. This knowledge comes through management. The productivity of identical technology varies with management procedures and how the know-how is transferred. In the case of integrated circuits, even with the same technology, the usability of product can range from 15 percent to 80 percent.

AMERICAN PARTICIPANT. China should learn, as did Japan, how to adapt foreign technology to fit local conditions, instead of insisting that the technology fit the conditions before buying it. Japan was also willing to buy older technology that was cheaper and established.

AMERICAN PARTICIPANT. The experience of Latin America in acquiring foreign technology through licensing has not been very successful. Japan had a trained, skilled labor force that offered the preconditions for using licensing successfully, and it might not have benefited from direct foreign investment. Licensing requires indigenous skill and know-how in putting together a package, which China may lack.

Excerpt from the paper by Rachel McCulloch

AMONG THE issues raised about the transfer of technology from advanced to developing nations, that of inappropriate technology is among the most controversial. Multinational corporations develop new production technologies primarily for use in the industrialized nations. Thus, almost by definition, such technologies are likely to be inappropriate to the conditions of China or other developing nations. However, research and development already performed represents a sunk cost, and existing technology can sometimes be applied at relatively low additional cost, although this need not be the case. Then a trade-off occurs between performing further R&D to tailor products or processes to Chinese users and incurring higher economic and social costs through use of available but inappropriate technology without modification.

This situation suggests that foreign investors unconstrained by local policies will not typically choose production technologies ideally suited to the low labor costs or other special conditions of the Chinese economy. Rather the production techniques employed will be a compromise based on technology readily available from use elsewhere but with some adaptations to local conditions. This technology is, however, economically appropriate, given the cost of performing additional R&D. It might be termed inappropriate only in the sense that a product or process developed de novo for the Chinese economy would have different characteristics.

The choices of foreign investors may be further tilted toward inappropriate technologies by some aspects of local policy. The Chinese law on joint ventures requires that workers in joint ventures be paid a premium over the wages paid by state-owned enterprises in the same area. The joint venture law also specifies that the foreign partner must provide technology and equipment that are "truly advanced and appropriate to China's needs." Like other nations' prohibition on importation of second-hand machinery, China's requirement of truly advanced technology and equipment is likely to promote the use of newer and almost always more capital-intensive production techniques. However, the additional requirement of appropriate technology poses a potential contradiction. How this aspect of the law is interpreted in practice remains to be seen.

High capital requirements characterize one type of inappropriate technology. Perhaps even more inappropriate for a country with China's scarcity of skilled technical workers are technologies that require large inputs of skilled labor. Even in the skill-abundant

United States, lack of complementary human resources has been the chief bottleneck to successful absorption of computers in industry and business. While U.S. and Japanese suppliers are understandably eager to accommodate the current Chinese enthusiasm for computer technology, the potential pitfalls in this area are formidable.

Comments

CHINESE PARTICIPANT. The question of appropriate technology varies from region to region and must be seen in light of the interests of the whole country and not of any particular province, county, or city. China has the additional problem of how to transfer technology from the developed regions to the undeveloped areas.

CHINESE PARTICIPANT. What technology is appropriate is different for each industry. Steel is not a new industry for China, but it needs new technology to catch up with Japan. China needs technology that can reduce energy consumption and improve quality. Appropriate technology means technology that is suitable to our situation. We need more computers and advanced technology for the whole country, but we do not need the most advanced technology, which we cannot absorb.

CHINESE PARTICIPANT. The most advanced technology is not the most desirable for China, because it is designed to suit the factor endowments of the developed countries: less labor and more capital. China wants technology that requires more labor and less capital. China has three requirements for the technology it imports: it must be useful to China, it must be profitable, and it must be unknown to China. If technology is already known to us, why should we have to import it? We must only import what is new to us.

CHINESE PARTICIPANT. There is no contradiction between advanced and appropriate technology; the two should be combined. If a technology is appropriate to China, it is already backward. Where does China put its emphasis? Principally on energy and transportation and on the upgrading of old technology. China also needs computers, electronics, and state-of-the-art technology but will not emphasize them.

In 1983 the United States called China a friendly, unallied country and allowed more electronics and technology to be exported to China. But sales must still get approval from the Coordinating Committee of the NATO countries.[3] The United

3. The Coordinating Committee of the NATO coutries, plus Japan and minus Iceland, oversees the export of strategic goods to communist countries.

States has not done enough to ease the committee's rules. France, England, and West Germany asked to have China removed from the restricted list, but the United States refused.

Implications for the Region

Comments

AMERICAN PARTICIPANT. What are the implications of the emergence of China for political relations in the Asian-Pacific region? Charles S. Pearson's paper gave me a new conceptual framework with which to analyze the problem of economic relations in East Asia. China may find a vacant rung between the NICs and ASEAN, rather than moving onto an already crowded rung. Earlier, one of our Chinese colleagues suggested that each rung is wider so that, as the range of products expands at each level of product sophistication, there is more room to stand. Taiwan and South Korea each have a foot on two rungs, so it is time for them to step up, leaving more room for China.

AMERICAN PARTICIPANT. China is not on an empty rung but one that is filled by ASEAN, Africa, and Latin America. This crowding is forcing Taiwan and South Korea to move up. They are being pulled into new opportunities for profit at higher levels even as they are pushed off the lower rung. It is true that we are adding rungs to the product ladder. The challenge for the United States is to add rungs quickly enough to keep its comparative advantage.

Excerpt from the paper by Wang Zengzhuang

CHINA'S OPEN economic policy, of which the importation of foreign capital and technology is an important part, is oriented toward the entire world, particularly the Asian-Pacific region. Countries and areas in this region are China's principal trading partners and major sources of foreign investment and technology transfer. China attaches great importance to strengthening economic and technical cooperation with them. As its open economic policy is implemented further, China's external economic ties, especially her economic and technical cooperation with other members of the Asian-Pacific region, will be expanded and reinforced steadily. The increasing economic prosperity of China, whose population accounts for half of that of the region and almost a quarter of the world's people, will in its turn contribute to the peace and security of the Asian-Pacific region as well as of the world.

Excerpt from the paper by Xu Jiewen

NATURALLY, the progress of China's economic relations will also involve China in the competition of the world market. But this position will not harm the economic development of other countries, and in particular it will not harm the economic progress of the developing economies. China is a developing country, and China's trade with other developing countries is mainly so the countries can supplement each other's needs and support each other. All countries, including those who produce the same type of products, for example, labor-intensive ones, have their particular comparative advantage because of the differences in their respective geographic locations, natural resources, industrial foundation, technological strength, and cultural background. At present, China cooperates with and complements other countries. It has not yet reached the stage of competition. Under such circumstances, China's participation in the international market will help all other countries display their strong points to offset their weak points, thus enhancing their economic effectiveness.

Most of China's foreign trade is conducted within the Asian-Pacific region. China's three major trading partners, and six of its top nine partners, are located in this region. In 1983, 54.4 percent of the total volume of China's import and export was with countries and areas in Asia. China's trade within the Asian-Pacific region also increased at a quicker speed than with other regions. For example, from 1978 to 1984 Sino-U.S. trade volume grew from more than $1 billion to more than $6 billion (U.S. currency), an average annual increase of more than 34 percent. Therefore, China's economic prosperity and growth in trade will benefit the economic prosperity of the Asian-Pacific region most of all.

Excerpt from the paper by Rachel McCulloch

THE FUTURE economic and political consequences of facilitating the emergence of a dynamic new competitor in world markets is a potentially important concern. With the world trading system currently strained to its apparent limits by the export growth of a number of much smaller newly industrialized countries, the potential role of China in international markets is viewed with some trepidation. Not only direct competition with producers in the advanced nations is relevant here, but also competition with established NICs that have strong economic and strategic ties to the advanced nations. If China's full integration into the world economy triggers a further increase in protectionism, the attractiveness of new export-oriented investments will obviously be lessened.

Comments

AMERICAN PARTICIPANT. In the past, the potential for China's trade was limited because it was a poor, centrally planned, continental country. Even though China is getting rich and moving away from central planning, its size is a constant. As development occurs away from the coast, the output produced along the coast will be sold inward rather than being exported. As countries get richer, the share of trade to GNP drops. Thus, when China reaches the GNP level of South Korea (about $2,000 per capita), I would anticipate that its trade would constitute about 8 percent to 12 percent of its national income. The world can easily accommodate that much trade, which is the equivalent of four contemporary Koreas. The issue is less the volume of trade than the way in which its direction and composition are determined. It could be disruptive if China goes through rapidly alternating periods of liberalization and protectionism in import policy. On the export side, if decisions are made on the basis of market considerations, all manufacturing sectors will have a share of China's exports; but if the decisions are made by central planners, then there will be huge exports of only a few items that will disrupt world markets.

Excerpt from the paper by Robert F. Dernberger

THE FUTURE development of China's economy will have little impact on China's present economic relations with the economies of the Asian-Pacific region. First, despite the changes in economic policies, strategies, and institutions, and the resulting changes in economic performance, China will remain a poor, developing country for some time. Western journalists, serving as modern-day Marco Polos, catch the reader's eye by describing the wonders of the new China as if it were about to become a capitalist economy, a modernized giant, and consumers' paradise. Yet even in an article that describes the current period in China as another of those "second foundings" in China's long history—periods of great glory, power, and wealth, which follow periods of ruthless repression—Robert Delfs states an important fact most clearly: "Against the sometimes dizzying sense of possibility inspired by the recent pace of reform, it is important to remember that many aspects of China's situation will be extremely resistant to change. China remains an overpopulated and desperately poor country."[4]

Thus in its economic relations with the other countries of the Asian-Pacific region China will continue to play the role of an

4. Robert Delfs, "On the Road to a Second Founding," *Far Eastern Economic Review* (March 21, 1985), p. 63.

exporter of agricultural and primary products, textiles and other processed agricultural products, and manufactured goods at the lower end of the range in quality and performance. The difficulties in expanding these exports to its major trading partners—all are in the Asian-Pacific region—are well known, already encountered, and will continue to limit China's capacity for export. I do not believe the present reform program will lead to dramatic changes in China's economic relations with the economies of the Asian-Pacific region compared with those that have already been established. China has already rejoined the world economy as a result of the economic reform program now under way, an event that was truly unexpected by those making forecasts just ten years ago. The near future, at least, should see the steady increase and consolidation of China's position in the world economy. One could spell out various dramatic and alternative scenarios, but the mere continuation of the trends in China's economic development and role in the world economy that have already been established as a result of the economic reform program will be dramatic enough.

Comments

CHINESE PARTICIPANT. Sino-Japanese relations are good, and growth has been steady and healthy. China is satisfied with its relations with Japan, but has three complaints. One, Japan has had a trade surplus in two of the last three years with China. The surplus in 1984 was $1.2 billion by Japan's estimate and $2 billion by China's count. The 1985 surplus is estimated at about $1.7 billion.[5] China's trade policy is a combination of trade and technology transfer, but Japan mainly pushes goods for which there are no markets elsewhere, such as electric appliances. A few years ago, the Japanese needed to import so much coal that China could not fully supply their request. Later, Japan wanted to cut down on China's energy exports by placing conditions on the quality of oil and coal imported from China. Imports of raw silk and textiles also have stringent restrictions. Japan wants to export cars and steel—China is presently the number one importer of Japanese steel—but this situation cannot continue.

Second, Japan has been less forthcoming than the United States in its technology transfer to China. The EC has been even more forthcoming, leading China to import much more technology from Europe. Japan is reluctant to transfer even the simple technology used in making household appliances. In joint ventures,

5. The actual surplus in 1985 was $8.2 billion by Japan's estimate, and $9.1 billion by China's.

Japan contributes some production lines, but the key equipment must be imported from Japan.

Third, although Japan has lent China a lot of money, it has not been willing to invest in China. Investment requires profit, so the flow of Japanese capital has been mainly to the United States. Japanese investments in China are aimed at opening the domestic market. The portion yielded in the domestic market to foreign investment was small at first, but since 1983 it has expanded. Japan saw it was falling behind and therefore made some concessions, explaining that its lag was partly because of difficulties in its decisionmaking process. An agreement on Baoshan was delayed because Japan refused to transfer technology. West Germany was then willing to transfer the technology that Japan was not. So Japan has also begun to make more investments—the amount more than doubled in 1984 compared with 1983. Japan also does not understand the Chinese system: the Japanese ask about autonomy in decisionmaking about labor, and they request guarantees for the supply and acquisition of resources, but a centrally planned economy makes the distribution of resources difficult and buying abroad wastes foreign exchange. Energy supplies are a problem for new enterprises. Japan is especially interested in areas they used to occupy, such as Dalian and Yantai. But the problem is still Japan's reluctance to transfer technology. They would rather sell us diapers and sewing machines.

Thus China's dissatisfaction with Japan has been over the small levels of investment and technology transfer provided by Japan and to a lesser extent over Japan's closed markets. Nonetheless, owing in large part to geographic proximity and cultural affinity, Sino-Japanese relations are in one of their best periods in history. I am optimistic about the continuing prospects for Sino-Japanese relations, but I would not characterize this development as a breakthrough if only because China cannot depend solely on Japan in its foreign economic relations.

CHINESE PARTICIPANT. Why are there so few Japanese investments in China? One reason is that China has not perfected its legislation. Another reason is that our infrastructure is still being built up. Japanese entrepreneurs want to invest in China but hesitate, as do other entrepreneurs. Japan is also worried about the boomerang effect of creating competition for itself. The United States is more farsighted and realistic and for that reason tops the list of foreign investors.

CHINESE PARTICIPANT. I am cautiously optimistic about Sino-Japanese trade, more so than some of my colleagues. There have been signs of progress on technology transfer and the increase of China's exports. But many problems remain. In trade, China has a large deficit with Japan. Last year it was $2 billion; China's total trade deficit last year was $1 billion. Clearly, our trade surpluses with other countries compensate for our deficit with Japan. China does not require trade balances in the bilateral sense, only in the aggregate. But if one deficit is quite large it requires that a surplus be maintained with all other countries. As for China's dependence on Japan, if trade is more balanced, the rate of increase is not a problem. Only if the imbalance continues is it a problem. China's share of Japan's overall trade is very limited, about 4.2 percent, but China is already a large market for Japan's exports. The United States is Japan's largest export market, but China is now second in terms of yen, although in dollars, exports to South Korea may be larger. Japan has the need to expand its market in China, but the question persists, what will Japan import from China? If it only imports energy and resources while exporting manufactured goods, the prospects are not rosy. The structure of trade needs to be changed to accommodate the import of more manufactured goods from China. This situation is related to the issues of technology transfer and investment. If Japan can make some changes in these areas, then the prospects are comparatively optimistic.

AMERICAN PARTICIPANT. I agree with the view that Sino-Japanese relations will grow without a breakthrough. Even though Japan is not now interested in importing Chinese energy, interest in energy development will grow. Concessional loans have been given for excavating coal mines and building transportation links to China's ports. The largest investment has been in oil exploration in the Bohai Gulf. Japan lagged behind in joint ventures until recently. Besides the general reluctance in Japan over technology transfers, the Baoshan episode caused a loss of confidence. Since 1983, however, a change of attitude has occurred in Japan. Might this not lead to investing in Chinese industries to gain access to markets, as was done in South Korea and Taiwan? Trade with Japan already accounts for 20 percent of China's total trade. How much of an increase does China hope to achieve? There must be some point beyond which China feels dependence on Japan will have gone too far. On the whole, China's fear of bilateral trade imbalances inhibits overall trade with Japan.

AMERICAN PARTICIPANT. Trade with Japan is already growing at 20 percent each year. How much more do you need to call it a breakthrough?

AMERICAN PARTICIPANT. There is potential in Japan for even greater trade with China. For one thing, if the United States gets its financial house in order and lowers its budget and current account deficits, then the pressure is on Japan to find new ways of sustaining growth. The Japanese government is not in a position to stimulate the economy through fiscal means, and monetary policy is not an option for them because they are already very liquid. It is not likely that simply lowering the interest rate would stimulate investment; indeed, if Japan thought it would stimulate investment it would lower the rate because it is an administered price in Japan. Export-led growth would cease in Japan, and that has been the source of as much as 40 percent of its growth in recent years.

Further, a sort of Japanese "Dutch disease" resulting from past lending abroad is going to take place. In the past, the current account was in balance, but a trade surplus occurred because of a deficit of services. But the large amount of investment Japan has made in the past, particularly in the United States, is going to yield a return flow of interest and some dividends. The future current account surpluses will produce pressure on Japan to run trade deficits to get any kind of sensible balance in its accounts.

So you have an economy that has been geared to export sales and not domestic sales, and a government that is not in the position, or does not believe it is in the position, to stimulate the economy. Pressure comes from all over to open markets, and Japan is reluctant to do that. That is when it will turn to China. In Japan, pressures may be building up for a dramatic increase in trade with China and for more willingness to lend and invest there, all for the purpose of having an export surplus with China that Japan finances itself. Japan will see China as a large market for its exports but will not willingly increase its imports proportionally because pressures for increased imports will come from all over.

AMERICAN PARTICIPANT. Could trade with Japan exceed 35 percent of China's total foreign trade?

CHINESE PARTICIPANT. Trade with Japan now constitutes about 25 percent of China's trade. In Japan's total trade, trade with China is only 4.2 percent. There cannot be much of an increase because all of China's trade partners want to increase trade, but China's capacity to trade is limited. There will be little increase in the percentage of trade with Japan.

AMERICAN PARTICIPANT. Institutional and political change happen very slowly in Japan, so any increase in trade with China will have to happen because of some change in fundamental, underlying economic forces. If the exchange rate changes dramatically over the next few years, Japan's ability to export to China would weaken significantly, and China's competitive position in exporting its manufactured items, the only area capable of expanding rapidly, would improve. We have talked about possible increases in exports of energy, but China needs most of its energy resources. The potential is in manufacturing, in which China has its principal comparative advantage. Japan might resist this picture, but China could be very competitive here, and one can anticipate substantial rises, if not in the ratio of exports plus imports over GNP, certainly in the proportion of China's exports to Japan to its imports from Japan.

Implications for Relations between the United States and China

CONFERENCE participants generally agreed on the increasingly positive, mature, and rational relationship evolving between the United States and China. Issues such as U.S. protectionism that limits imports of Chinese textiles, restrictions on the technology that can be legally transferred to China, a continuing American trade surplus, and differences over Taiwan still greatly concern both countries. The conference also noted the relative decline in the importance of strategic and military issues in U.S.-China relations and the rise of the economic dimension in Sino-American ties.

The Expansion of Trade

Comments

AMERICAN PARTICIPANT. Two different intellectual perspectives have been brought to these meetings. One is the bargaining perspective: two sides fighting for their own interests through an adversarial process. This posture comes naturally to lawyers, who seek to protect the different interests of their clients. Diplomats and those trained in Marxist dialectics also favor this stance. But it creates problems when used in trade relations. The modern economist has a different perspective: if you have well-functioning markets, all will benefit and living standards will improve. Trade relations are not adversarial because trade is not a zero-sum game, but a positive-sum game.

Which view dominates the dialogue on trade issues? If it is the bargaining perspective, then the developing countries ask the United States to open its markets, make more concessions, and do more to assist them. The United States will not be persuaded and will ask, "What's in it for me?" The moral claim is that the developing countries are poor and need help, but by that logic the United States will help Africa and Bangladesh, not Singapore and China. A better argument is that if the United States ignores the Asian-Pacific region it will harm its own strategic interests.

81

But the most persuasive case is neither political nor moral, but economic: free trade provides cheaper goods for consumers, offers an outlet for U.S. agricultural surplus, and creates competition, which improves productivity in American industries. All countries benefit from technology transfer—even the United States receives some technology from Japan. The argument against free trade is that the adjustment process harms the poor, but this is not, on balance, a persuasive justification for protectionism.

Historically, the bargaining perspective has dominated U.S.-Japanese relations because the Japanese, especially the policy-makers, do not believe in the liberal tradition. They have made all concessions grudgingly under U.S. pressure. This attitude plays into the hands of the United States, since many of the negotiators in trade talks are lawyers who enjoy the adversarial process and do not understand economics. This state of affairs has contributed to increased protectionist feelings around the world.

Whether U.S.-China relations will follow the path of U.S. relations with Japan (arguments over dumping, protectionism, and the like) or be different depends on several things. First, what will the pace of the growth of trade be on the Chinese side? If trade grows from its current level of $30 billion by 10 percent a year, which is less than China estimates, in seven years it will be $60 billion and in fourteen years, $120 billion. This is a large trade volume and will be greater if Hong Kong is included. South Korea and Taiwan will continue growing at the same time. In a very short time, China will not be playing only a small role in the world market. Second, protectionism may not become a serious issue because the pace of Chinese imports will grow as fast as its exports. China, unlike Japan, will not have surpluses, which do not make much sense for Japan and certainly do not make any sense for a developing country like China. Third, no matter how extensive China's reforms, they will not go far enough to have a positive role in reducing protectionism in China. For instance, the United States cannot complain to Hong Kong about trade restrictions because Hong Kong plays by the rules of pure free trade. If the United States violates those rules, the onus is clearly on the United States. But no matter how far the reforms go in China, trade will continue to be under some central control and protection, so tension over China's closed market will continue. At most, China may open to the same degree as Japan did in the 1950s and 1960s. In this respect, there is some reason for feeling that U.S.-China relations are similar to U.S.-Japan relations, and therefore some cause for pessimism arises. Finally, on the American side, a future recession would lead almost certainly to protectionism, which would exacerbate economic tensions between China and the United States.

CHINESE PARTICIPANT. Sino-American economic relations have developed in a fairly smooth fashion: trade has grown rapidly and U.S. investments in China have increased. But obstacles to the relationship remain. China is also a developing country, therefore, the problems of developing countries also apply to China. There is also the Taiwan question.

U.S. protectionism has had an impact on China, especially on textiles. Chinese exports have increased in recent years, but during the first quarter of 1985 there was an absolute drop. Some local Chinese leaders are upset not only with the United States but also with the central government for not taking a tougher position in opposing American protectionism. Many restrictions on the export of advanced technology have been relaxed, but many still remain, as American companies will testify. We hope for further improvements in this regard.

Excerpt from the paper by Mao Yushi

THE UNITED STATES has the most powerful economy in the world while China has the biggest population. But Sino-American economic exchange, measured either in trade or in investment, is very limited. Bilateral trade amounts to a mere 1 percent of the total U.S. foreign trade and one-thousandth of the U.S. GNP. For China, it represents only 10 percent to 13 percent of the country's total foreign trade, and 1 percent of GNP. This abnormal phenomenon is the result of the absence of contact between the two countries for thirty years after China's liberation in 1949.

To the benefit of both sides, Sino-American relations were normalized in 1979. China's recent policy of opening to the outside world and stimulating the domestic economy has brought about drastic changes in its economic structure and institutions. In this context, bright prospects have been opened up for Sino-American trade. Between 1979 and 1984 the total volume of two-way trade reached $28.2 billion, with the United States enjoying a surplus of $5.82 billion. China's ongoing economic readjustment will continue to make its influence felt in Sino-American trade.

Grain used to be a major American export to China. In recent years, however, China's grain production has exceeded its domestic consumption and is likely to continue to do so. We estimate that the required annual growth of grain production for the coming fifteen years will be only 2.9 percent. Such a rate is the same as the average in the period 1952–84, and far below the figure of 5 percent registered in the 1978–84 period.

Moreover, the production cost of grain in the United States may not necessarily be less than in China. As the role of energy, chemical fertilizers, and pesticides in grain production is much greater in the United States than in China, the production cost of American grain will decrease as a result of the slump in oil prices. Even so, economic analysis may show that grain imports from the United States will not be a welcome proposition in China. Despite China's scarcity of farm land, the cost of grain production is low, thanks to an abundant labor supply and the use of labor-intensive techniques of production. It is, therefore, reasonable to predict that Chinese imports of American grain may decrease or even become unnecessary in the years ahead, except in case of bad weather in China.

The other side of the coin, however, is that any possible downward trend in grain imports will be more than compensated for by the rise in the purchases of U.S. high-tech products. Following President Ronald Reagan's order of June 1981 to relax controls over U.S. technology transfer to China, trade in such products increased to $900 million in 1983, or 40 percent of the total U.S. exports to China in the same year. This was three times that in 1982. In 1984 the value of exports of U.S. high-tech products to China doubled again, to $2 billion.

China's import capacity depends not only on the level of economic development but also, and more directly, on the country's current account. Unless Chinese goods and services enter the world market, China will have no international purchasing power at all, however rich it may become. Therefore, the key to future Sino-American trade lies in the amount of Chinese goods and services that can be brought into the world market, expecially in the United States. The export volume per capita of Singapore, Hong Kong, and China's Taiwan province reached $9,000, $4,500, and $1,400 respectively in 1983, while for mainland China the figure was merely $25.

It is true that the U.S. government has expressed readiness to expand trade with China but, owing to the protectionist pressure of the U.S. textile industry, it has put up obstacles to U.S. imports of Chinese textiles. This is self-contradictory, indeed. Sales of Chinese petroleum products, the largest item after textiles, may decline since China's vigorous economic growth is causing the domestic demand for such products to mount as never before.

China's other exports to the United States are scattered among various categories, none of which appears likely to take off in a major way. This means that both countries have yet to explore the areas in which China can expand exports. Such efforts will have a close bearing on the further development of bilateral trade.

Direct U.S. private investment in China totaled only $700 million by 1984. This represented merely 2.3 percent of all U.S. investment in the Asian–Pacific region, and less than 1 percent of the total figure for American investment abroad. Calculated another way, the sum of U.S. investment in China in the past five years was less than 1.5 percent of China's domestic capital investment for the single year of 1984. What is gratifying is that the situation has changed for the better in the last two years, and a rapid increase has taken place in the number of investment projects agreed upon by the two sides.

Excerpt from the paper by Wang Zengzhuang

OVER THE last few years, the United States has made considerable progress in transferring technology to China. By implementing an open economic policy, China has done much to import foreign capital and advanced technology. The United States, in recent years, especially in 1983, relaxed restrictions on technology transfer to China. Thus conditions for the further development of bilateral technical cooperation have been created. With the relaxation of U.S. policy on technology transfer to China, such transfers are on the increase both in volume and in technological level. For instance, the United States has exported technologies used in China's construction of some key projects, such as the joint exploration of offshore oil and joint development of coal mines and the technologies used to help some old enterprises and to fill certain gaps in China's know-how. The United States has also introduced advanced managerial skills that are useful in training Chinese personnel in industrial organization and management. At the same time, however, some U.S. legislation discriminating against China is still in effect. Applications for permission to export technology to China, which conform to the new regulations of the U.S. government, have met with willful obstruction or long procrastination. Furthermore, the U.S. stipulation that the granting of most favored nation status to China must be reexamined and approved by Congress each year has made it difficult for the two sides to work out long-term plans for economic-technical cooperation. Such obstacles must be removed through the efforts of both sides if their economic and technological cooperation is to expand.

Comments   CHINESE PARTICIPANT. I agree with my colleagues that Sino-American economic relations have been satisfactory. The trade volume has increased, and the United States has eased somewhat its restrictions on technology transfer. Before 1984, the United States was ahead of Japan and Europe in investments in China. The trade volume for the first quarter of 1985 was $1.7 billion, compared with $1.4 billion for the same period in 1984. U.S. exports to China increased by 24 percent and imports by 16 percent, so the United States still has a surplus. But from another perspective, we are not fully satisfied. The first reason is the issue of the trade balance: Chinese exports have increased, but textiles are down; only oil and oil products have increased. Traditional exports from China have also been restricted and unilateral cancellations of contracts by American businesses have occurred. China's capacity to pay will be adversely affected by these types of actions. Another reason is technology transfer: although restrictions have been relaxed, problems still remain and there are no economic reasons for these restrictions. The Coordinating Committee of the NATO countries has already been mentioned, and the scrutiny of contracts by the U.S. Department of Defense is also a problem. The United States also interferes in technology transfers from third countries by regulating the exports of the foreign subsidiaries of American firms.

The development of Sino-American economic relations does have an impact on Sino-American political relations and is conducive to the improvement of those relations, but in the end they are two different things. Political obstacles still slow the growth of economic relations. From the strategic and security point of view, China feels the only threat it faces is the Soviet Union. The United States is not a threat, and China is in no position to pose a threat to the United States. The Taiwan question still exists, and it inhibits political and economic relations. The United States and China both have firm positions on these matters, but if they abide by past agreements, then progress is possible.

Political Dimensions

AMERICAN PARTICIPANT. The overall trend in U.S.–China economic relations has been positive. Political relations have facilitated, and in turn have been helped by, economic relations. The key variable is the Taiwan issue: while it has been placed to the side for now, it will be crucial to the further development of Sino-American ties.

The military-strategic dimension is more problematic. The United States and China have an implicit strategic relationship, but explicit strategic or military ties are subject to severe limits. One limit comes from the Chinese side: even though the Soviet Union is the principal enemy, China pursues an independent foreign policy and will not be an ally of the United States. Another limit comes from those on the American side who want to restrict the extent of the military relationship with China. Because both sides pursue strong bilateral relations for strategic reasons vis-à-vis the Soviet Union, some observers in the United States believe that a military-strategic relationship is necessary for sustaining the overall relationship. These people must be convinced that economic and political ties are sufficient to sustain Sino-American relations. The United States and China do not need a military relationship. Arms sales to both Taiwan and China are too complicated to go very far down that road.

AMERICAN PARTICIPANT. The emphasis placed by both sides on the military relationship has declined in relative terms, and the relative importance of the economic relationship has increased. The long-term effect of this shift is uncertain. Clearly, tensions are likely to occur between the United States and its trading partners on many issues, especially if the U.S. economy begins to slow. At the same time, the euphoric talk of a close quasi alliance with China against the Soviet Union was unworkable and is now fading. Since this concept was an unsustainable base for relations in the first place, I see the shift in focus from strategic to economic considerations as a positive and necessary trend.

Second, a normalization of the relationship has occurred. Now the two countries deal with a wider range of contacts and issues. In the beginning, four people (Mao Zedong, Zhou Enlai, Richard M. Nixon, and Henry A. Kissinger) controlled the entire relationship. Now government agencies, economic enterprises, research institutes, and families interact.

The China lobby no longer monopolizes the China issue. At the beginning of the relationship, tremendous pressure arose to improve relations with China by giving it special treatment. The past tendency was to deal with China as a separate case, but now issues affecting the United States and China are handled as part of the regular policymaking process. The nuclear cooperation agreement is a good example: China was not singled out for discrimination but was subject to the same political processes and pressures as would apply to a nuclear cooperation agreement with any other country. The same can be said for the textile issue.

The wider range of contacts makes for a healthier, more normal relationship, but it also creates the possibility for more tensions. This situation leads to the issue of "maturity" in the relationship. The Chinese do not like this term because to them it signifies biological maturity, meaning that the relationship has grown to its fullest extent. But to the United States it means psychological maturity: the ability to deal with problems in a calm, level-headed way without exaggerating the difficulties. By this definition, the relationship is mature, and the groundwork has been laid for solving future problems.

There are two ways, suggested by this conference, for dealing with problems. One is the consultative process, of which this conference is an example. The more opportunities for informal, unofficial dialogue, the more chances there are for identifying problems before they get too serious and for finding ways if not to solve them, at least to manage them. Another alternative, as some of the American participants have suggested, is for China to become involved in the American policymaking process. China should try to influence policy, not simply wait and react to it.

CHINESE PARTICIPANT. Trade problems between the United States and China need to be resolved through bilateral negotiations. The Western countries are comfortable with the political relationships among themselves, but numerous contradictions arise that require consultations along the lines of the seven-country summit talks. Such contradictions also exist in Sino-American bilateral relations. Our complaint is the unilateral actions and the cancellation of contracts by the United States. The agreement on 6 percent growth under the multifiber arrangement violates the bilateral Sino-American textile agreement, and the country-of-origin rule was made unilaterally. It is unfair to China and is not conducive to the growth of bilateral trade. If the United States cancels contracts, perhaps it feels its house is stronger and can withstand retaliation by other countries. Perhaps the United States feels it will benefit from its protectionism more than it will be harmed by protectionism from Asian-Pacific countries.

AMERICAN PARTICIPANT. Most Americans feel it is appropriate that the United States has lost its political-economic-military dominance of the 1950s. The question today is what will replace American dominance. If many small military powers emerge, confrontation, individual protectionism, and isolationism will arise. China's involvement in the world is therefore one of the great events of the end of this century because it fights this trend. China will be a large, industrialized country, regardless of whether it will become a newly industrialized country or not. Will China be concerned only with its self-interest, as the Soviet Union has been? It is also important for the U.S. economy to remain open, in part to facilitate the opening of China's market. China also needs to be open. Not everybody in either country agrees on this point. Therefore, it is important for people like us at this conference to go on fighting the good fight.

CHINESE PARTICIPANT. I would like to suggest two other ways for countries to handle their relations. One is for each country to think only of its short-term interests. The other approach is for the countries to think of their long-term interests together.

Protectionism, from any perspective, is not a good idea. I agree that it would be best for the United States to remain open and for China to become more open, but at least in the United States, the tendency to become more protectionist remains. It has been suggested at this conference that protectionism will probably become more serious. If this is so, I would say the prospect for cooperation in the region is not very optimistic. So I am greatly puzzled when my American friends are pessimistic about limiting protectionism but remain optimistic about future cooperation in the Asian-Pacific region. If we do not try to alleviate the trend of protectionism, it is impossible to have cooperation in the region. I certainly agree that we, as scholars, should do our best to work for an open market in the United States and for an outward-orientation for China.

Conference Participants

People's Republic of China

Pu Shan
Director, Institute of World Economics and Politics
Chinese Academy of Social Sciences

He Fang
Director, Institute of Japanese Studies
Chinese Academy of Social Sciences
Paper: "The Japanese Economy and the Asian and Pacific Regions in the 1980s"

Wang Zengzhuang
Research Fellow, Institute of International Studies
Paper: "Technology Transfer in the Economic Development of the Asian-Pacific Region and China"

Xu Jiewen
Associate Research Fellow, Institute of Economics
Chinese Academy of Social Sciences
Paper: "The Reform and Prospects of China's Economy"

Gu Yuanyang
Associate Research Fellow, Institute of World Economics and Politics
Chinese Academy of Social Sciences
Paper: "Economic Development in East and Southeast Asia and Its Trends"

Mao Yushi
Associate Research Fellow, Institute of American Studies
Chinese Academy of Social Sciences
Paper: "The U.S. and Asian-Pacific Economies—and Their Relationship"

Wang Dingyong
Assistant Research Fellow, Institute of World Economics and Politics
Chinese Academy of Social Sciences
Paper: "Trade in the Asian-Pacific Region and Trade of Labour-Intensive Products in the Region"

Liu Xihan
Research Assistant, Institute of World Economics and Politics
Chinese Academy of Social Sciences

Zhang Tong
Interpreter, Institute of World Economics and Politics
Chinese Academy of Social Sciences

90

United States

A. Doak Barnett
Professor of Chinese Studies, Johns Hopkins University
Senior Fellow Emeritus, Brookings Institution

Ralph C. Bryant
Senior Fellow, Brookings Institution

Robert F. Dernberger
Professor of Economics, University of Michigan
Paper: "The Chinese Economy: The Awakened Dragon?"

Bruce Dickson
Research Assistant, Brookings Institution

Harry Harding
Senior Fellow, Brookings Institution

Lawrence B. Krause
Senior Fellow, Brookings Institution
Paper: "The Economies of East and Southeast Asia: Mainly Success
    Stories"

Robert Z. Lawrence
Senior Fellow, Brookings Institution
Paper: "Issues in American Economic Policy"

Edward J. Lincoln
Research Associate, Brookings Institution
Paper: "Future Prospects for Japan and Implications for the Pacific
    Region"

Rachel McCulloch
Professor of Economics, University of Wisconsin at Madison
Visiting Scholar, Hoover Institution
Paper: "Technology Transfer to China: The Role of Direct Foreign
    Investment"

Charles S. Pearson
Professor of International Economics, Johns Hopkins University
Paper: "Asian Exports and Footwear Imports"

Dwight Perkins
Professor of Economics, Harvard University

Thomas W. Robinson
Professor of Government, Georgetown University

WIDENER UNIVERSITY
WOLFGRAM
LIBRARY
CHESTER, PA.